From **Darkroom** to **Dugout**

My Adventures Photographing Springfield Cardinals Baseball

By Mark Harrell

Foreword by

Josh Kinney, Former Springfield, and St. Louis Cardinal.

Library of Congress Control Number: 2019901682

Name: Mark Harrell

Title: From Darkroom to Dugout: My adventures photographing Springfield Cardinals Baseball / Mark Harrell

Description: Memory Burn Creative LLC

Additional copies of this book may be purchased on DarkroomToDugout.com

Printed in the United States of America

ISBN: 978-0-578-46199-1

Thank you to Josh Kinney for writing the Foreword for this book.

Front cover photo: Springfield Cardinals pitcher Jeremy Cook is ready to deliver the first pitch at Hammons Field in Springfield Cardinals history. Photo taken my Mark Harrell.

Back cover photos clockwise:

Double play at home plate: Photo by Mark Harrell

Matt Carpenter: Photo by Mark Harrell

Xavier Scruggs walk off homerun on July 4th: Photo by Mark Harrell

Catcher Andrew Knizner: Photo by Mark Harrell

2012 Texas League Northern Division clinching game: Photo by Mark Harrell

Allen Craig during Texas League All Star Game homerun derby: Photo by Mark Harrell

Group photo of Matt Pearce, Austin Gomber, Sandy Alcantara, Dakota Hudson, and Jack Flaherty: Photo by Mark Harrell

Stan Musial throws out the first pitch in 2005 while Matt Gifford watches: Photo by Mark Harrell

McGwire homerun held by Megan Harrell: Photo by Grant Allen

Old train photo: Photo courtesy of Richard Crabtree

All photos taken unless indicated were taken by Mark Harrell.

Table of Contents

FOREWORD

By Josh Kinney

When I was climbing through the minor leagues on my way to the major leagues, having my picture taken for a baseball card, or actions shots didn't mean all that much to me. I was too busy giving it my best so I could realize my lifelong dream. I did achieve my dream in 2006 by becoming the first Springfield Cardinal to be called up to St. Louis. It was good timing because the following year I pitched in the NLDS, the NLCS and the 2006 World Series, winning a World Series ring after the Cardinals defeated the Detroit Tigers four games to one. Now that my career has played out and I am no longer a part of major league baseball, I appreciate the mementos of my playing days. It has become special now, since my three sons; Saxton, Sawyer, Swayde, and my daughter Star were born. I can pass down those memories to my kids, and their children.

I remember those early days with Springfield well. The great crowds. Great fans. Some of my fondest memories are from my minor league days. All the teammates and coaches I met along the way. It was cool to meet so many fans, staffs, grounds crews, isle attendants, and many more who all had a common love for baseball. Hammons Field was brand spanking new and baseball fever was at a high pitch. It had been decades since the last minor league team played in Springfield and the city was more than ready to embrace a team once again. Springfield, Missouri is most definitely Cardinals country. One person I got to know was team photographer Mark Harrell. He was knowledgeable about baseball, plus he took our photos. That is a good combination. It is fortunate for Springfield that they have someone who had a sense of history when it is happening and can capture it for future generations to see.

I married a local girl and have put down roots in Southwest Missouri. My kids like going to watch the Cardinals so we jump in the car once in a while and go watch Cardinals baseball at Hammons Field. When I walk into the clubhouse area to visit, I enjoy looking at the photos hanging up, reminding me of guys I played with and the excitement of the future, and what it had to offer. I am also very proud to be a little part of Springfield Cardinals history. I am the first Springfield Cardinals player, to become a St. Louis Cardinal. Now that is a pretty good trivia question to ask someone!

Mark's book is a great way to preserve not only Springfield Cardinals' history, but Cardinals Nation history for future generations. I know former Springfield players and fans alike will get a kick out of reading this book. He makes it fun to travel down memory lane with humorous stories as well as photos that many players and fans have never seen. Springfield is a loyal St. Louis Cardinals town. I'm glad my time in Springfield has been preserved by Mark's photos and stories!

CHAPTER 1

HOW'D YOU GET SUCH A SWEET GIG?

Often people ask how I got such a sweet gig with the Springfield Cardinals as their official photographer. It is a sweet gig, but it comes with a price. Extreme cold, hot temperatures, rain delays, tornado warnings, tend to be hard on cameras and even worse on old photographers. There have been many family outings, birthdays and missed vacations because the Springfield Cardinals had a game or home series that overlapped. If there was a game scheduled, I wanted to be there. I do it because I love it - pure and simple. If a picture is worth a thousand words, then I have about 364 million Springfield Cardinal words on my computer's hard drive. My guess is I have shot about 910 games and averaged around 400 photos per game for 14 seasons.

Sometimes a picture is only worth deleting. An umpire blocks the shot. A baserunner bolts in front of the camera at just the wrong time. Or, as you are taking a photo and counting to three, somehow people's eyes are still shut. There have been thousands of photographs suffer the fate of my dreaded delete button. To be sure there have been some shots worthy of being mounted and framed. Some of those shots are currently hanging in the hallway leading to the Springfield Cardinals Clubhouse. There are several of my photos hanging on those walls, which I will get to a little bit later. It's been an interesting journey these last 14 seasons. My dad suddenly passed away in October of 2006. Five years later mom passed away in 2011. The St. Louis Cardinals, the team I live and die for, won the World

Series both those years. I'd like to think it was God's way of easing my pain, just a little bit.

Over the past 14 seasons I'd like to think my technical camera and computer skills have evolved into being functional enough to handle the latest and greatest editing software and digital cameras. The cell phone camera is still a struggle though. The Cardinals keep me inspired to be committed to keeping up with the latest technology, although it is getting harder and harder to do so. It seems like every week there is a new update, upgrade, or up-something. A few talents I have refined out of necessity are editing in Adobe Photoshop and Lightroom. Just as importantly, I've taken gigantic leaps forward in organizing large quantities of photos into a manageable process.

In the beginning, because I was new at shooting hundreds of photos in a short time, I stored the folders on my computer in random places with random titles. That led to hunting the images down, much like looking for a needle in a hay stack. I'd open a folder, look though the thumbnails and close the file. I had to repeat the process until I found the photo I was looking for. It took me awhile to realize that there were more efficient ways to store photos. Now, I create a new folder for each game and name the file after the date and year of the game. In addition, I will create a folder for each individual player. Folders are stored in two separate places. one being in the "cloud" for safe keeping. Now, if my computer crashes, or a tornado blows it away, there is still a copy of all my folders in the "cloud".   In the long run being organized will save a photographer a lot of time. It's so frustrating looking for an image and not be able to find it. Several media outlets request photos from me. I'm a regular contributor to the St. Louis Cardinals Game Day Magazine. They have a huge readership, so it's always nice to see an occasional photo of mine in the magazine. Steve Zesch with Game Day Magazine will email photo requests asking me for shots of top prospects. When I know a player is going to be featured, I will give him a little heads up that they are going to be in the next edition. When I deliver the news, I mention that in all the years I have been contributing photos, there have only been a couple players who didn't make it to the major leagues. That usually gets a pretty big smile out of them. It takes time to read the writers email request, find the photos, attached them to the email, and send them out. Now I don't cringe when I get a request because I am organized.

In 2016 I passed all the requirements to be an FAA Part 107 Small Unmanned Aircraft Systems licensed drone pilot. I enjoy flying drones and earning money. In my real, 12 months out of the year job as a business owner, I offer clients photography, video, drone footage, virtual tours, website, and graphic design. My time with the Springfield Cardinals has been a life changing experience. This experience was something I sort of stumbled into. I wasn't qualified for it, but I didn't let that stop me.

Here's a funny story. When the St. Louis Cardinals announced that they were moving their Double A team from Sevierville, Tennessee to Springfield, it was very disappointing to me. The future of the Ozark Mountain Ducks, an independent baseball team, was doomed the minute that announcement was made. It hit me hard. For several years I had been everything from a photographer, batting practice pitcher, to play by play radio announcer for the Ducks. Now they were toast. My shot at being

El Fenómeno

In 2012, Oscar Taveras won the Texas League batting title and was the Texas League Player of the Year and Cardinals organization Player of the Year. Above he is holding a feature article written by Cardinals Game Day Magazine. There are several photos of mine that they used for the story. I had Oscar pose for me before a game holding open the article.

In 2014, Taveras homered in his major league debut against the San Francisco Giants and went on to hit .239 in 80 regular season games. I covered an inter- league game in Kansas City the week after he hit his first homer. Before the game he came over and said hello. I told him Springfield was very proud of him. I commented that his homer against the Giants was awesome. He smiled and thanked me. That would be the last time I would ever speak to Oscar. I heard the news during Game 5 of the 2014 World Series that he and his girlfriend had been kiled in a car wreck in Puerto Plata, Dominican Republic.

around baseball up close and personal had come to an end, or so I thought. Initially, I told myself that I might not ever go to a Cardinals game after what they did to my Ducks. Things changed when I started reading about all the amazing things that were going to happen at Hammons Field when they arrived. So, what the heck, I decided to offer my photography services, as suspect as they were, to the newly formed Springfield Cardinals, the Double A Texas League affiliate of the St. Louis Cardinals.

I didn't think I had much of a shot at getting the gig. I didn't have an expensive camera, let alone a set of lenses that I would need for different conditions. There are a lot of lighting and weather conditions that I would eventually learn how to deal with. In 2005 the digital camera was still in its infancy. I was lucky enough to have a nice Nikon D1 camera, which was a pretty good camera back in the day. I had bought it cheaply for $750. That turned out to be a good investment for me. The D1 sold for $5,000 when it was new. It captured a 2 mega pixel file size, which was not too bad for that time. To show you how far the digital camera industry has come, my Nikon D810 shoots 36.3 mega pixels. Some digital cameras shoot much larger file sizes than that. Those additional pixels add detail to the images. It eliminates the grainy look when you enlarge an image too.

In 2005 my memory card for the D1 held 256 meg of memory. That much memory would hold about 400 pictures shot in basic mode. Now I use a 64 gb card which holds thousands of photos in normal mode. I had been a photographer for several season for the local independent baseball league's Ozark Mountain Ducks. Early on with the Ducks I used film to photograph the game with, 36 exposures per game. After each game I would show up at our local Walmart photo lab and drop off the game roll of film. If there were 10 good photos out of the roll of thirty six frames of 35mm film I felt like I had a good night. The Price Cutter Park lights weren't that powerful, so I didn't have a fast lens to help compensate for the lack of light. I guess I shot enough good ones because they kept me around. I certainly didn't have a photography degree on the wall, or even photo credits. I did gain some valuable experience shooting for the Ducks. Not only did I learn how to shoot baseball in the evening, late hours, but how to build relationships with players, fans, and management. I had been a yearbook and newspaper photographer for the Kickapoo High School journalism staff. I cut my teeth developing film and prints, going to events with a press pass, and making deadlines. Thankfully, because of the Ducks I had a baseball photo portfolio to show Mike Lindskog, the new Springfield Cardinals Broadcaster & Public Relations Manager. I did have ONE major advantage over all the other photographers who were interested in becoming the Official Photographer of the Springfield Cardinals. I wanted it so badly I could taste it. And I was willing to do it for free that first year, much to the chagrin of my wife Wendy.

In my defense, there wasn't a budget for a staff photographer anyway. The agreement was that the Cardinals would give me a press pass that would allow me to come and go as I pleased. I could choose the games I wanted to shoot and in exchange I would let them use my shots as they desired.

In the beginning there was no way of knowing how addicted I would get to being close to the game. The agreement was that I would be their go-to photographer if they needed something. From the first year on I have always been most accommodating to the club if they needed anything. After that first year I developed an agreement for online sales of game day shots with the team. That agreement is still relevant. It allows me to invest in better equipment which produces better images. I am a business man, with a lot of sales experience. I knew that the building of relationships with staff, sponsors and fans would far outweigh what I might earn per game, as needed, basis. Without trying to sound too cocky, there is another advantage I had over other photographers. Baseball has been a part of my life since I was old enough to open a pack of baseball cards. I had played baseball through high school and men's leagues. I also played AAA fast pitch softball for several years. Springfield was pretty darn competitive from the1960's through the 1980's. I was pretty sure I knew the game of baseball better than any of the other photographers, and probably some of the sports writers too. I called the Cardinals and got an appointment with Mike Lindskog.

Mike had been the radio play by play person for the El Paso Diablos of the Texas League and now he was in his new position. He was a nice, trendy young guy and was very pleasant. He reminded me of TV host Ryan Seacrest. We met in the new clubhouse lounge for about 30 minutes. After going over all my reasons for wanting to shoot for the Cardinals, he smiled, shrugged his shoulders and shook my hand and then said, "Looks like you are our photographer." I'd like to think I won him over by telling him how I truly love the game of baseball, and will do a great job for them, not to mention my very impressive 8 x 10 glossy portfolio samples, albeit slightly out of focus.

That first year was a trade out, my time and photos for a great seat in the house. It reminds me of the story legendary announcer Bob Uecker wrote in his autobiography "Catcher in the Wry". He said when he was 18 years old, he signed a contract with the Milwaukee Braves for $3,000. He said his dad was very angry with him because they didn't have that kind of money to spend. I sort of fit that scenario. Yes, this newly minted title of Official Photographer of the Springfield Cardinals was a game changer for me, with no pun intended.

During my time with the Cardinals I have had the privilege of meeting people whom I would never have had the opportunity to meet - local media, sportscasters, weathermen, newspaper writers, mayors, politicians, and local celebrities. The Springfield Cardinals are such a high-profile icon in Springfield they attract a wide variety of people each season. When I show up at Hammons Field for a game, I never know who might come out of the crowd and say hello. There have been several former school chums, some all the way back to Holland Elementary grade school whom I haven't seen in years. They will stop me and say hello. It gets a little awkward when a person asks if I remember them. Sometimes I don't. Some people I have not seen in more than 50 years. There are occasions when a parent or parents of my old friends will say hello, although that generation is starting to fade away and the next generation (mine) is assuming the role of grandma and grandpa. School teachers and coaches, old neighbors, and former co-workers tug at me as I run by and say hello. Without my opportunity to be at the Cardinals games, out in view of the public for all to see, running around the field, sweating, running stairs to

Various Media

Jay Fotsch with Power 96.5 has been on-field host since 2008.

Joe Daues 2005. Former KOLR

Christine Daues 2005. Former KY3

Julie Wilson FOX 5

Kevin Howard KGBX-FM. First' Public Address Announcer. Kevin ran the P.A. for all or parts of the first 6 seasons.

Tim Tialdo

Jeff Houghton
The Mystery Hour

capture a certain photo, I more than likely would have never seen or spoken to many of my old acquaintances ever again.

There have been many "this is your life" moments. It's fun when famous people, whether it be a local TV celebrity or a nationally known figure, shows up to a game. Usually if they are there, they will be throwing out a first pitch or taking a tour. That gives me an opportunity to spend a little time with them. The last thing I want to be is a pest so I usually introduce myself and let them know I will be taking a few photos. They know I am with the team and it gives them a sense of comfort. Often people will be waiting in line to speak to the celebrity so I just sort of hang around and don't butt into conversations.

There have been some notable people that have graced our beautiful ballfield. I've met several baseball Hall of Famers, such as Red Schoendienst, Lou Brock, Bob Gibson, Ozzie Smith, Steve Carlton, Bruce Sutter, Tony La Russa, Whitey Herzog and Jim Palmer. Politicians include Former United States Attorney General John Ashcroft, two sitting Missouri Governors, Matt Blunt, and Jay Nixon, plus a sitting United States Senator, Roy Blunt. There have been several Congressmen, actors, singers, professional golfers, bull riders, authors, NFL players, NBA players, pro tennis players and even game show host Bob Barker. There's one fellow that my old high school chums and I have argued about for a couple years now. They were sitting on the front row on the Cardinals side when I stopped by to say hello. The seventh inning stretch started and a group of singers from Branson started singing God Bless America. There is one singer that looked A LOT like Bill Murray, the comedian, and movie star. He is known for doing crazy

MLB Hall of Fame
first pitches

HOFer Bob Gibson signing a ball for Chris Maloney (Mgr)

HOFer Lou Brock visiting with Ron Warner (Mgr).

HOFer Ozzie Smith with Matt Gifford.

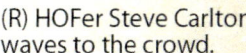

Above: Ron Warner, Mgr. greets HOFer Bruce Sutter

(R) HOFer Steve Carlton waves to the crowd.

things like showing up at places randomly. None of the Springfield staff was aware that Murray was in attendance. I snapped a photo with my cell phone. I went online and found several photos of Murray. I still think it was him. Maybe, or maybe not.

Sometime celebrities will walk in unannounced. One time I was sitting around the visitor's dugout snapping away when I noticed a unique looking fellow all by himself watching the game. In my mind I thought "that guy looks like John Goodman a little bit". But this guy is smaller in stature and older looking. I snuck a couple photos of the man with the intention of showing people how much this guy looks like John Goodman. When I showed one of our isle attendants, he laughed and said "that IS John Goodman. He is in town for a Missouri State University Tent Theater production". Goodman is an alum of Missouri State and attends a Cardinal game every year or two. Our fans leave him alone and he appreciates it. People are just people. Celebrities put their pants on just the same as everyone else. Like my old Kickapoo High School baseball coach John Rottenberry used to say, "Boys those Hillcrest players put their pants on one leg at a time". I yelled out "Yeah coach but have you seen the size of those legs?" He got a kick out of that. But, to say I don't get a little bit of a treat out of meeting celebrities would not be accurate. Being able to see many of these people behind the scenes does make you realize they really are just human. People with World Series and Hall of Fame rings. People with big bank accounts. People with awards and honors. People who get paid to sign their name on memorabilia. There's a pretty good chance I will never be paid to sign my name at a card show, but I do have some minor league hall of fame stories to share. Some are funny. Some are sad. The intention of this book is to give you a little bit of behind the scenes, and behind the camera insight into why being a team photographer for the Springfield Cardinals is a dream come true for me.

CHAPTER 2

MY BASEBALL ROOTS RUN DEEP

For you to understand what makes me want to show up at
the ballpark for the last 14 baseball seasons, day in and
day out, for very little money, to photograph baseball, let
me enlighten you. Baseball is my love. It is my friend. It
represents my youth, and my adulthood. Baseball has
always been a big part of my family history. My uncle, Bob
Speake, played 4 years in the major leagues. He is one of
the first Springfield born and raised boys to make the
major leagues. He also has the distinction of playing with
the Springfield Cubs. For a year or two, the Chicago Cubs
had a minor league team that played on the west end of
Springfield. Bob got to sleep in his own bed on home
games which was rare for a minor league player in those
days. When I was very young, my family would visit Uncle
Bob and Aunt Joanie at their home on East Lombard St.
Three doors down lived an old grizzled ex-catcher by the
name of Mickey Owen. At that time Owen was Greene
County Sheriff. But he made his name not as a sheriff, but
as a major league baseball player. Mickey played in the
days of the old Gas House Gang. Uncle Bob told me a story
about a time he was in the minor leagues, playing first
base for the Des Moines Cubs. Des Moines happened to be
playing an exhibition game against the parent club, the
Chicago Cubs. Mickey Owen had been in the majors since
1937 and was sort of hanging on trying to land a spot as a
backup catcher with the Cubs. Owen was catching that
exhibition game against Des Moines. Mickey was friends
with my grandpa, Jim Speake, who was a good baseball
player himself. When Bob came to bat the first time up,
Owen squatted down and flashed a sign to the pitcher,

My uncle, Bob Speake, holding up his 1957 Topps baseball card.

Springfieldian Mickey Owen

and promptly whispered "SPEAKE, a fastball is coming down the middle." My uncle didn't really know Owen, but knew he was friends with grandpa. It was Mickey's way of taking care of a fellow Springfieldian. The fastball came in, Speake swung, and hit it over the fence. Now even if you know a fastball is coming, you still have to have the talent to hit it, let alone hit it over the fence. The home run put Uncle Bob on the prospect map.

Almost 65 years later my uncle still tells that story with appreciation in his voice. Bob retired from professional baseball after the 1959 season and went into the bowling alley business, opening Holiday Lanes in Springfield. My grandmother ran the front desk at the lanes, keeping a watchful eye over her son's business. My sister Linda and I would bowl all day on Saturday for free. I was barely big enough to get the ball down the lane, but I loved it.

Another Springfieldian, Sherm Lollar, a catcher primarily for the White Sox, also owned a bowling alley in Springfield. It was a trend in the 1950's and 1960's for major league players to own bowling lanes and hang out in the off season, attracting bowlers who also happened to be baseball fans. Lollar was a very good catcher for the White Sox and was their everyday catcher for most of the 1950's. Sherm had a few autographed baseballs in a case by the front desk in his bowling alley. One ball was from the 1947 Yankees team that Lollar played for briefly. He had the unfortunate task of trying to beat out another rookie catcher by the name of Lawrence Berra, who would later be better known by his nickname, Yogi.

Lollar also had in the display case, one of his three Gold Glove Awards he won as catcher. I remember my parents bowling at Lollar Lanes when I was little. When my parents were bowling, I was hanging around the front desk eyeing the memorabilia of an actual, real live, major league baseball player. On top of that, he lived in Springfield.

In the mid 1960's I went to my first American League game with uncle Bob and my three cousins. The game was between the Kansas City Athletics and the Minnesota Twins in old Municipal Stadium. Al Worthington, an old San Francisco Giants teammate of Bob's, was still pitching in the big leagues for Minnesota. Before the game Bob walked down to the railing and started talking to his old teammate. My uncle knew how I worshiped baseball, so he waved me over to him and introduced me to Worthington. I was shaking. A real major leaguer in full uniform shook my hand.

I tasted success on the baseball field from an early age. My dad coached my Kiwanis youth teams. I was our only pitcher. There were no rules back then limiting how many innings a kid could pitch. I am lefthanded, threw strikes, and was a fairly hard thrower on top of that. I could hit a little too. We didn't have tournaments and tons of travel games like they do now, although I wish they would have. Our team was lovingly called "F Troop", after the 1960's TV show about a bunch of mis-fit Calvary soldiers. We won first place five or six years in a row. In 1967 I was selected to win the A. W. Briggs Sportsmanship of the Year for my age bracket. With that award came a trip to New York City to watch the Yankees play. The funny thing is, I am a lousy sport; a terrible loser. But we won every year, so I guess I looked like a good sportsman.

Here is the J. W. Briggs Sportsmanship award for the Downtown Kiwanis Baseball League given to me in 1967. I represented the Bantam League 11 to 12 year old boys.

My family took a trip to California on a train like the one above to visit my aunt. 1967 was the last year of passenger train service to Springfield. We left Springfield on a two day journey. There were no sleeping coaches. Everyone slept in their seat. That was a long trip.

Our host for the trip was my grandpa Speake's buddy, Mickey Owen, who I mentioned earlier. Owen was one of the original Springfield Cardinals when he played for the 1935 team. As excited (and scared) as I was to go see the Yankees, there was a conflict in my schedule. Not that I ever had much of a schedule at 11 years old. But, yes, a conflict. My family had planned a trip to California to visit my aunt Betty, my dad's sister. The train tickets were already purchased. I had to turn down the New York trip and go to California. That was the first time I had ever left Missouri.

We took a passenger train out of Springfield. That was the last year of the passenger train in Springfield. When you see an old black and white movie of people on a train, it looked exactly like that. It was a two-day ride to Los Angeles. We went to Disneyland, Knott's Berry Farm, the Hollywood Wax Museum. My dad took me to Malibu Beach where I saw my first bikini. Now I know why it was just him and I that went. Even though California was amazing, I regret not going to New York. To this day I could kick myself for not going on that trip to Yankee Stadium with Mickey Owen. I was told later that he was able to take the boys fortunate enough to make the trip into the Yankee clubhouse before the game. They got to meet several of the Yankee players, including Mickey Mantle.

Baseball has always been my first love. I played baseball for Kickapoo High School. It's the same high school that actor Brad Pitt attended a few years later. He was a better actor and I was a baseball player. My senior year I was selected as an Ozark Conference outfielder and team MVP. I also made two American Legion All Star teams. Once as a pitcher and the other as an outfielder. I played 3 years of varsity baseball. In fact, I was on the very first Kickapoo baseball team to ever play back in 1972. Our team stat guy was a fellow classmate of mine by the name of Rob Rains. Rob wore thick glasses, and just looked the part of a future sportswriter. We both were in the same journalism class. He, as a reporter, and me as a photographer. Do you see a pattern beginning here? Rains went on to become a respected and accomplished major league baseball writer, based out of St. Louis for most of his career. He was elected into the Missouri Sports Hall of Fame in 2017 for his outstanding journalistic work. Rob invited me to attend so I took photos of his induction and happily gave them to him. He has written several books, mostly with a St. Louis Cardinals baseball theme. After we graduated from high school, Rob moved away from Springfield and I rarely saw him. Other than a class reunion or two, that was it.

A few years ago, Rains had written another book and had traveled to Springfield to promote it. He was scheduled to throw out a ceremonial first pitch during one of our pre-game ceremonies. I ran into him during pre-game and we started to reminisce. He told me after pre-game he was going to sign books in front of the Team Store for a few innings. He suggested that I stop by the press box later in the game so we could catch up on all the latest classmate gossip. It was his turn to throw the pitch, so he was marched out to the pitcher's mound. The public address announcer introduced him and encouraged fans to buy his book up on the concourse where he would gladly sign it. I snapped the picture of him in mid-throw. We exchanged emails and I told him I would send him the photo, and that I would make it up to the press box around the 5th inning to chat. The next day I emailed Rob his first pitch picture. I didn't see him again for some time. After watching Rob promote his book, it made me start thinking that maybe I had enough experiences with the Springfield Cardinals to write a book. At least it now it was planted into the back of my mind. Rob still had roots in Springfield. His mother was living in Springfield which gave him the opportunity to check on her, and at the same time catch a Springfield Cardinals game. Rains started a website, STLSportsPage.com, that features St. Louis sports with a heavy emphasis on Cardinals coverage.

As his website grew, Rob started writing stories about top prospects within the Cardinals minor league system. It was easier for him to come to Springfield to interview players because this was his hometown and it is just a three-hour drive from St. Louis. He started frequenting Hammons Field more often. Rob would text me and let me know when he was going to be there. We started meeting up in the press box during the game and chat. As time went on and our meetings increased, our conversations about reminiscing of high school faded away and was replaced with insider Cardinals baseball talk. Any time he was writing a feature on one of our players, I would send him a few photos of that player for him to use.

After about my eighth season with Springfield, I felt like I had enough stories to write a book. There were certainly plenty of photos to back up the stories that were to be told. After jotting down a few of my memories, the process of reminiscing started appealing to me. When Rains came to town for a game early in 2012, I told him that I wanted to write a book about my experiences, but I'm not sure anyone would read it, including my family. Rob told me to send him a few samples of stories and he would give me his honest opinion. That night I emailed a few stories to him, holding my breath in anticipation. He was gracious enough to give me a quick response. Rob said "yes, I think you have a book. Use lots of photos and mention St. Louis people, so you will capture the St. Louis market as well. Then he said, "if you need an editor, I would be happy to do it." That was all I needed to hear.

CHAPTER 3
SHOCK AND AWE

Pre-season exhibition games with the St. Louis Cardinals are a special treat. Those games are held at Hammons Field with about the same frequency as a presidential election, every four years or so. The first two exhibition games in Springfield Cardinals history are the most memorable to me by far. I was a rookie photographer. I didn't know what to expect. The games had been super hyped by the media and fans were whipped into a frenzy with anticipation. It was the hottest ticket in Springfield since Elvis played Hammons Student Center in 1977. After a mostly sleepless night due to excitement, I woke up early and got ready for the early afternoon game. I drove into the front office parking lot where there was a parking attendant checking credentials. Hanging from my neck was my temporary paper press pass. I happily flashed it and smiled. The attendant just waved me forward, which gave me a real feeling of being somebody. When I walked through the office doors, I checked in with a staff person in the lobby. She gave the nod to go on through the office and out to the field. I pinched myself to see if I was awake or dreaming. Here I was, walking through the Springfield Cardinals office on my way out to the field for the first time as the official photographer of the Springfield Cardinals. The year was 2005. Coming to town were the 2004 National League Champion St. Louis Cardinals. All of their famous players were making the trip to Springfield - Albert Pujols, Scott Rolen, Jim Edmonds, Larry Walker, David Eckstein, and a very young and untested Yadier Molina. Tony La Russa, the future Hall of Fame manager would be piloting the club once again that season.

Where it all started...

Chris Maloney, manager of the Springfield Cardinals
and Tony La Russa, manager of the St. Louis Cards
on opening day 2005.

Yadier Molina signing autographs on day two.

Yadi, after hitting a homerun, is greeted by Jose Oquendo. Notice that Molina's number is 41. It was later changed to #4.

Molina catching 2nd day of exhibition games.

Pushing the glass double doors open, I took a hard right to an open gate down the right field line. It was sunny, but cold, with zero wind. If you were in the sunshine, it was nice, but if you were in the shade, a winter coat was needed. The grass had a bright and beautifully saturated green appearance. The seats were dark green, and the sky was robin egg blue. There was a sparkle to the entire facility. If there is a baseball park in heaven, and I hope there is, it would probably look like Hammons Field did that day. The field was empty when I made my first trek towards the Cardinals dugout. As I approached it, I realized there were two men sitting on the bench talking. One man was immediately recognizable. It was Tony La Russa. The other fellow was wearing a Springfield Cardinals uniform. I assumed it was their new manager, Chris Maloney. La Russa and Maloney got up from the bench and started walking up the steps towards the field. Maloney was pointing out things of interest to Tony about the field.

My first act as team photographer was to get up enough nerve to go over and introduce myself. After swallowing hard, taking a deep breath, I walked up to the two managers, shook their hands and introduced myself. I asked them if it would be too much trouble for me to get a couple of shots of them together? Both managers were very accommodating. After the first shot Tony realized he had sunglasses on. He said, "Oh wait, let me take my glasses off". Maloney had sunglasses on as well and he took his off too. I took another snapshot without their glasses on. Those two photos represented my first photos taken as a Springfield Cardinal.

Maloney started giving Tony the grand tour, so I walked away happy that I had gotten those shots. I decided to snoop around and get familiar with the landscape. There's a concrete entrance down the left field side that I figured had to be the visitor's clubhouse. It would be a good place to get a glimpse of some of the St. Louis players. I walked through the concrete passage way, then opened the door and saw the clubhouse boys getting ready for the St. Louis players to arrive. It was like walking into my own personal baseball fantasy. Each locker had a jersey hanging from it. Red lockers with beautiful white jerseys with birds on the bat. That was a sight to behold. I took photos of those hanging jerseys making sure to get the number 5 Pujols jersey. As time has passed, making a poster of those hanging jerseys seems like something fans would love to have.

It was time to work my way back to the field and see if any Springfield players had made an appearance. There were a few players stretching and getting ready to jump into the batting cage. Not one of those players looked familiar to me. Some of the guys looked like they were fresh out of high school. When batting practice started, management opened the gates early to give fans a sneak peek into the future of Cardinals baseball. As the baby birds were swinging away in the cage, most fans were not into it. They wanted the BIG club to take batting practice. We really didn't have any huge prospects on that first Springfield team. The News Leader had written a story about one of the Cardinals young minor league players, Reid Gorecki. He was selected in the 13th round of the 2002 Major League Baseball draft by the Cardinals. Reid was the closest thing we had to a golden boy on the roster. Other than Gorecki, there were no other players on the prospect radar. Springfield teammates had taped the News Leader article on Reid's locker, teasing him for being in the spotlight. In

Reid Gorecki found this article taped to his locker
by some of his fun loving teammates.

Visitors locker room before first exhibition game in 2005.

2005
Springfield Cardinals players and coaches arrive for the first time at the Springfield Regional Airport. They represented a new era, ushering in professional baseball in Southwest Missouri.

Early fan favorite Reid Gorecki, being interviewed by local media.

Players loading their gear into the team bus baggage bay.

2005

Chris Maloney managed Springfield to a record of 70 wins and 70 losses.

Catcher Robinson Cancel was a Texas League All Star. Later in his career, he played for the Brewers, Mets, and Astros.

Travis Hanson was a Texas League All Star.

Tyler Mingus hit .324 with 19 homeruns. He was a Texas League All Star.

2004 St. Louis had ranked near the bottom in producing minor league prospects. St. Louis strategy for several years was to spend big money on proven major league free agents or, by trading away their young talent for veterans. With a rare exception they didn't rely on their minor league system to populate the parent club roster.

 The Cardinals strategy kept them in playoff contention most years. The previous year, St. Louis had played in the World Series against the Boston Red Sox. They were swept in four games and it was Boston's first World Series triumph since 1918.

When the day started, I was among those fans pulling for the big club against Springfield. It's funny now, because I have grown to love the Springfield Cardinals, front office staff, current players, formers players, coaches and managers. They are all like family to me now. If you cut me, you will see that I bleed SPRINGFIELD Cardinal red. But back then I was like everyone else. St. Louis was king. When we have an exhibition game against the parent club now, I always root for the Baby Birds.

During the last part of Springfield's batting practice, the big club had started their slow walk to the front of their dugout to stretch. They were shaking hands with media and the like along the way. That normally would never happen during the season but during an exhibition game, rules can be bent. Soon they got down to business. Pre-game preparation is a very repetitive process - stretching in groups, playing catch in small groups, as well as taking batting practice in small groups. Selection of groups are determined by who is in the starting lineup and who's in a reserve role that day. Scott Rolen and Albert Pujols started

Albert Pujols taking batting practice at Hammons Field. He hit a ball three-fourths up the scoreboard in centerfield during b.p. I have never seen another like it in fourteen years with the Cardinals. Playing arm chair quarterback, I was way too close to the cage for taking photos. A foul ball would have shattered my camera.

Scott Rolen taking swings in the cage.

Jim Edmonds during batting practice.

Albert Pujols hitting into a net with the assistance of coach Hal McRae.

hitting balls off a tee into a small net that has been placed in front of the stands behind home plate. I'm glad now that I really didn't know my boundaries, because I shot some very nice, up close photos of those two All Star players. Those two men dwarfed others around the cage. Rolen was a mountain of a man and Pujols had muscles on top of muscles.

Springfield had just finished batting practice, so the cage opened up for the big boys. Dave McKay, the first base coach for many years under La Russa, made his way out to the mound to throw batting practice. Since there were no boundaries set to me by St. Louis, I thought to myself that I might not ever get a chance like this again, so I pressed up right against the netting of the cage and snapped away. A late swing causing a foul ball going into the net would have shattered my camera, but I was willing to take the chance. After all, I was capturing history. The first hitting group included Pujols. I will never forget the sound that his bat made when he made contact. It was different than anything I had ever heard up close on a ball field. The air seemed to get sucked out of the cage after each Pujols swing. It felt like the fillings in my teeth loosened up on every mighty swing too.

On about the fifth or sixth swing El Hombre crushed a pitch to straight away centerfield, striking the Coca Cola sign midway up the distant scoreboard. After 14 years of Springfield baseball I still have never seen another ball hit that hard or far up the scoreboard.

When the big club was finished with BP, they went back into the visitor's clubhouse to change into their game uniforms. Head Groundskeeper Brock Phipps signaled for

Springfield Cardinals team getting ready to be introduced to their fans for the first time.

Stan "The Man" Musial waves to the crowd. Stan threw out the ceremonial first pitch of Game One..

2005

Albert Pujols takes a mighty cut against Springfield.

Red Schoendienst exchanges lineup cards with Chris Maloney.

Opening Day
2005

Top: John Q. Hammons waves to crowd

Middle Left: Entertainer Andy Williams sings National Anthem

Middle R: Stan Musial plays harmonica with Matt Gifford watching.

Botom L: Louie helecopter ride introduction.

April 2nd, 2005
OPENING GAME:
Hammons Field

Springfield pitcher
Jeremy Cook
delivers a strike to
David Eckstein,
short stop for the
St. Louis Cards.
This is the first
pitch in the new
Springfield
Cardinals
history.

Cook checks the
runner Jim Edmonds.

Edmonds taking
imaginary swings in the dugout.

his crew to prepare the field for play. They started dragging the field and liming the baselines. Before long the field was sculptured into postcard perfection. By this time the crowd had swollen to a capacity crowd of about 12,000 rabid fans. There were so many fans you could not see a blade of green grass out on the grassy knolls which extended from mid-leftfield all the way around to mid-right field. Professional baseball in Springfield was about to usher in a new era.

I was standing on the track behind the on-deck circle on the Springfield side when a golf cart drove through the open wagon gate out in center field. It snaked along the warning track and a loud cheer began to rise into a roar. The PA announcer enthusiastically welcomed Stan The Man Musial as he made his way to the field to throw out the ceremonial first pitch. Springfield Cards Vice President and General Manager Matt Gifford escorted Musial half way out to pitcher's mound, with Matt giving him support as he slowly walked. It was an eye opener for me on just how time had passed. A true childhood hero of mine was now a fragile senior. Before Musial threw the pitch, he played "take me out to the ball game" on his famous harmonica. The crowd cheered enthusiastically. Soon afterwards, Andy Williams the singer of Moon River fame, beautifully sang our National Anthem. I was snapping away, nervous at the thought of missing an important moment. As the opening ceremonies ended, it was time for me to pick a place to photograph the game.

Every nook and cranny of both photographer's wells were crowded with media personnel. Each well is only about 6 feet by 8 feet in size. They are located on the first and third base side. An open spot still had not been taken on the third base side, so I hustled over to claim it. My plan was to make sure I didn't miss the very first pitch in the new Springfield Cardinals history. Jeremy Cook took his last warm up tosses and it was time to get down to business. Cook's first pitch was a strike to St. Louis shortstop David Eckstein. That moment in time, taken by my camera, will forever document the moment professional baseball came back to Springfield.

During the game I kept thinking that someday, maybe 50 years later, some kid who loves baseball history as much as I do might look and study these photos wanting to imagine what it must have felt like to have been there that day. As a student of history, I've always been fascinated with old photos. No doubt that fascination drove me to be a photographer. Journalistic photography is my passion. I've never been interested in artistic photography. I'm the type of person who wants to watch a documentary, not fiction. Covering events offer a front row seat, or a behind the scenes look at what truly is going on. Tom Mast, former local television sports anchor was visiting with me during a game up on the concourse. He looked at my Cardinals credentials hanging from my neck and commented: "Access is everything my friend." That is so very true.

When I was a kid and even to this day, I love to study and marvel at historic old photos of players like Babe Ruth, Cy Young, Ty Cobb or a young Willie Mays. Imagine what it must have felt like to have been there to see those baseball legends play in real time, in full color. Our first exhibition game saw St. Louis defeat Springfield rather easily. There wasn't a great deal of action by either team, but it didn't matter. Everyone knew that we had just witnessed a special moment in Springfield history. The first game was under my belt. But the job is not finished until the card reader goes into the computer and photos are stored in a safe place. Driving home there was the satisfaction knowing that if I got hit by a bus on the way home, at least I got to live out a dream for one day.

As I went down to my basement and pulled up a chair in from of my computer, I pulled the memory card out the camera and inserted it into the card reader. Soon the images popped up on the screen. The colors were so bright and beautiful. When you look at shots from an event, it's always smart to study them, and ask yourself if there was a better way to shoot next time? Would a different angle work better, or maybe shoot from the other side of the field? Where will the sun be in a certain inning? Is there a man on first with less than two outs and you want a nice double play sequence, you might focus on second base, hoping for a double play ground ball. I carefully saved the files to my computer to make sure they would not get erased accidentally. In addition, individual CD's were burned. I didn't trust my computer to be the only place to store this treasure. Game One images stayed on my memory cards for a couple years. Every time I thought about erasing them to make room for new photos, a little voice would say "What if I lose those images." That is always a photographer's worst nightmare.

There was still another exhibition game the next day, so charging batteries, and making sure there were enough memory cards was the plan for the remainder of the evening. Day two at the park found me once again, super early. The first day's experience had given me some confidence. The staff, players, and crew were starting to recognize me as one of them. That relaxed me a little and made me feel slightly more like I was part of the team. When I cover an event, no matter how big or important, I always like to get there early and be ready to shoot video or still photos. If there's an unplanned obstacle, I will have enough time to figure out a solution to the problem to either shoot around the problem or fix it. That way I won't miss the beginning of the event. There's nothing worse than a ceremony or event starting while I am still monkeying around, trying to fix a camera issue. One prime example of missing a shot for me came when John Q. Hammons, the namesake of our beautiful field and reason we have Cardinals baseball in Springfield, was being honored before a game.

For some reason I was running late. The presentation had not started, so I took my camera out of the bag, put the bag in the well and trotted towards home plate. Right when they were handing JQH his award, my camera indicated that the battery was dead. It was not dead because I had just charged it. Quickly I said to hold on for a second. I took the battery out of my camera and put it quickly back in. That is a trick that usually works, sort of like rebooting a computer. Still no power. I acted like I took the shot, everyone smiled and went their merry way. Running off the field now saying a few choice words under my breath, I jumped into the well, determine to find out the issue. As I turned my Nikon on, the camera lit up, just like it was supposed to. The battery icon indicated "full power". For whatever reason my camera did not want to take that picture. The good news is, to this day no one has ever asked for that photo. After 14 years, I think I'm safe. I did learn a lesson. Always carry a spare battery and memory card in your pocket during shoots just in case.

When I played sports, there was always a drive for me to get there early and not have to rush to put on a uniform or not have enough time to warm up properly. The same goes for event photography.

Exhibition Game Two: It was another chilly day in the Ozarks, but no one was complaining because the sky was as robin egg blue and baseball would be played. Weather in Southwest Missouri in late March can range from 60 degrees and sunny one day to 25 degrees with two feet of snow the next. The action of Game Two was more of what the crowd had hoped for. The St Louis bats came alive in a big way. Edmonds, Walker, Pujols, Rolen, Molina, and Hector Luna all hit home runs. Springfield got their hat handed to them this game. La Russa started subbing his starters in the fifth inning, giving non-roster players a little bit of playing time. As St. Louis players were subbed out of the game they slowly walked down the third base wall, signing autographs all the way to the visitor's clubhouse. That never happens in a regular season game. The players delighted the fans by signing autographs and posing for pictures. The big leaguers had a sense of history and could feel how special this initial series was. During the second game the first base well was my spot to shoot. There were not as many media types for this game as there were the day before, which was nice. From this angle I noticed while playing first base, Pujols would crouch low to the ground right before the pitch was thrown, reaching out his arms with glove ready for action. After watching him get ready for each pitch, I was impressed with how pretty the scoreboard was up against the blue sky. Pujols' uniform in the foreground completed the photo. I wanted to have a nice shot to prove future Hall of Famer Albert Pujols

2005

Reid Gorecki, Papo Bolivar, and Shaun Boyd pregame meeting.

Pujols, Isringhausen, Morris, Edmonds, Oquendo, and Rolen throw first pitches to Springfield players.

Larry Walker sliding into third baseman Travis Hanson's tag. Hanson would hit 20 homers for Springfield in 2005.

Hanson signs for a fan.

Long time KY3 sports broadcaster Ned Reynolds announcing the starting lineups.

Kevin Estrada was a solid gloveman in 2005.

indeed did play at Hammons Field. The best way to freeze time is to have the scoreboard in the background, with the clock, innings, count, etc. That way you know exactly when it was taken and at where you were during the game.

In 1998, my daughter Megan and I had made the trek to St. Louis for a September game. I had gotten the tickets months ahead so I had no idea at the time that Mark McGwire would be going for home run number 61 to tie Roger Maris' all time single season record. We were lucky enough to have good seats for that historic moment. I had an old Canon Rebel film camera that I brought with me to hopefully capture some history. This was before photography had become a big part of my life. In the first inning, Mike Morgan, pitching for the Chicago Cubs, served up number 61 to Big Mac. My camera was not very good. I didn't have a long zoom lens, so I was not able to zoom close to the subject. As the pitch was coming in, I pushed the shutter about the same time McGwire swung. The ball left the park like a rocket. Megan and I witnessed the tying of Maris' single season home run record. Never before or since have I experienced such a loud and emotional moment. When Sports Illustrated printed a special edition of McGwire's historic home runs, they included many photos. When you turn to number 61 you will see Megan and I in the background standing on our feet, cheering our hearts off, and me holding my pathetic camera. When I took my roll of film to get it developed, there was some nervousness as to whether there were any good shots of the record breaker. A protective green netting was in between our view of McGwire. My cheap camera was having a hard time with auto focus. It kept focusing on the netting and not McGwire. The auto focus would whirl and search for a subject to lock onto. I wasn't sure if I captured

To capture history you have to be in the right spot at the right time...

My daughter Megan, holding my photo of McGwire's record tying 61st home run.

a nice photo of McGwire, or a nice sharply focused photo of the protective net. That would be a mystery until I dropped off the file at the lab. The next day the lab handed me back my prints and the tech commented, "Looks like you got to see McGwire hit a home run."

Nervously nodding my head, I opened the envelope to view my prints. First photo, out of focus. Second shot, the net was in perfect focus, but McGwire was a blur in the back ground. Third shot, more focused netting right before he was getting ready to swing. The fourth shot was my money shot. Luckily McGwire was in focus and the netting was a faint image. In retrospect, it was fortunate that I did not have a zoom lens. If I did, I would not have captured that moment in history nearly as well. The picture could not have been timed any better. The ball was frozen in mid-air, just to the left of the scoreboard. The scoreboard had the time, inning, pitch count, 60 home runs for his total, and so on. If I had taken a close-up of Big Mac on that swing, people would have to take my word that it was record tying number 61.

There were thousands of photos taken that day of number 61. I'm guessing there were not all that many that validated the moment by having the scoreboard in the background. To this day, if there is something of significance happening, I try to put something in the background that proves it was taken at that particular moment. The shot of Pujols playing first base with the Hammons Field scoreboard in the background is a favorite of mine. It validated that El Hombre graced our ballpark. That particular shot has been hanging in the front office for 14 years now. I stop to look at it every so often. There are hundreds of people that have seen that photo. Visitors will stop and look at it on their way through the hall. The magic of those first two exhibition games will go down in the Springfield history books as among the most memorable city events ever. The Battle of Springfield, which was fought in 1862 during the Civil War, might be of more significance to the shaping of our city, but it sure wasn't as much fun as those two exhibition games played in April of 2005.

CHAPTER 4
HANGING IN THE HALLWAY

Occasionally someone asks me, "What is the most memorable photo I have taken during my time with the Cardinals?" To be sure there have been many. But the answer to that question might be surprising. It's not a photo of a famous person or an historic moment. The photo that I pick is based upon its uniqueness. It was taken on the last day of the 2009 season. The team did not qualify for the playoffs, so our players were just riding out the last game with bags packed ready to make the trek back home. It was a beautiful late summer day. When a team photographer is faced with shooting the last few games of the year they want to take as many shots as possible. That's their final opportunity until next spring. As a rule of thumb, a portion of players that are on the Springfield roster at the end of the season will come back to Springfield the following year. It's always nice to have some shots of each returning player ready for next spring if needed. There have been many times while sitting at my computer in the middle of winter that I realized I didn't take a shot of this person or that player. Most of the time it's because the player did not join the club until the last few games of the season. They may have mostly sat on the bench or perhaps it was a pitcher who worked an inning or two after I had left for the night. It's easy to miss late-season additions. Newspapers will contact me during the winter asking for photos of various players. When I hear a player's name that I don't recognize, there is a good chance it didn't get taken. Covering my bases with last-minute action shots is par for the course the last week of the season. Now, let's dissect this most unique shot.

31

It was taken in the top of the eighth inning. The crowd had started to thin out. I settled into an empty seat in the front row. It was just to the left of the protective net, safely hidden from the dangers of a foul ball. but close enough to lean over and get an unobstructed shot. By the eighth inning the temperature had risen into the upper 80's. I decided to celebrate the last couple innings with a cold beer. I can count on one hand the number of times I've bought a beer and watched a game as a spectator in this park. My camera was ready just in case some action might unfold in front of me.

We were playing the Angels' affiliate, the Arkansas Travelers that day. The Travelers had a rally going. With men on first and second, their hitter hit a soft sinking line drive to right center. Both of the Travelers base runners were not sure if the ball would be caught. They did what good base runners are supposed to do. They played it half way. Our right fielder, Tyler Hensley, dove for the ball to try and make the catch. He came up just short of making a spectacular snag. The ball squirted out of Hensley's glove and squibbed away. The runners were off to the races. Both runners misjudged just how far the ball had rolled away from Hensley. He bounced to his feet and made a strong throw to the plate. With heads down, steaming around the bases, both men decide that they could score. The lead base runner on second base had gotten a late jump on the play, and the man on first had one thing on his mind – he was going to score. As he was rounding third, he ran right through the third-base coach's stop sign and headed for the plate.   Both men come storming down the third base line, one right after the other. Hensley's throw was right on target, Steven Hill, our catcher, caught the throw just before the lead runner slid into his tag. Hill

My favorite photos taken at a Springfield Cardinals game.

Taken on the last day of the regular season 2009.

Steven Hill applies the tag while third baseman Joe Mather watches in wonderment.

tagged him out and less than two seconds later the runner who was on first was tagged out by Hill. If you are scoring from home, it was a 9 - 2 double play. Hill looked like a grocery store clerk who was scanning groceries as they went by on the conveyer belt. It was a most unusual double play and one I don't ever remember seeing in person, before or since.

Fortunately, I was in a perfect spot to get that sequence of shots. That evening when I downloaded my shots, I did a little fist pump celebration. I chose what I thought was the best photo of the sequence to make a poster. Our third baseman Joe Mather was standing on third looking home with a look of disbelief. Both Travelers runners were sliding into home plate at nearly the same time. Hill was applying the tag to the first on with the second runner in mid-slide, just a few feet back.

I liked that shot so much that I had a poster made of it and gave it to Scott Smulczenski for possible usage on the hall wall. Smulzy had the photo mounted and it has been hanging in the hall ever since.

There have been some amazing shots that sadly I've missed for one reason or another. But on that day, I captured a unique moment in Springfield Cardinals history. This shot is worthy of the hall.

The most historic shot that's hanging on the wall is the first professional pitch ever thrown at Hammons Field, which was the first exhibition game against St. Louis. Springfield pitcher Jeremy Cook is in the middle of his delivery getting ready to throw a strike to David Eckstein, the Cardinals' shortstop. At the bottom of the poster is a description of what the event was, for future generations to enjoy. Here is a funny story. In 2018 Eckstein came back to Hammons. There was a dinner in his honor being held after the season. As he was talking and signing autographs, I told Smulczenski that we should have Eckstein sign the wall poster. He smiled and said, "Good idea"! He went to grab it off the wall and take the poster out of the frame. As time passed, I began to wonder where Scott had gone. I wanted to present the photo to David and tell him the story behind the poster. I also wanted to ask him if he had any memories of that at bat. Eventually Smulzy came back into the room with no print to sign. He did have a funny look on his face. Curiously I asked where the print was. He said, "We are not having him sign it." I'm like "Why not?" He rolled his eyes, smiled and said, "You misspelled his name and left out the c in Eckstein". We laughed and then I told him we could have Eckstein insert the letter c with a Sharpie pen, and then sign it. He didn't buy that idea. All those years of hanging on the wall and nobody had caught the typo.

There are a couple of team photos hanging on the wall too. In 2005 we did a little re-creation of an old 1930's Springfield Cardinals photo. The players were walking along the baseline in a straight line three abreast. We had our 2005 players line up as best we could to mimic the old photo. Papo Bolivar, our left fielder, was instructed to lean to the right with his arms bent to mimic the old photo. He did a pretty good job of nailing the pose. It was used for a promotional piece. That was our first year and I really was timid about making many suggestions. I wanted to do a team photo of that group of guys but didn't want to overstep my boundaries. I wish now that I had been more forceful because we did not take a traditional team photo for a few years. It was not until 2008 that we finally took

Ky3 Sports Director Chad Plein, interviews Eckstein.

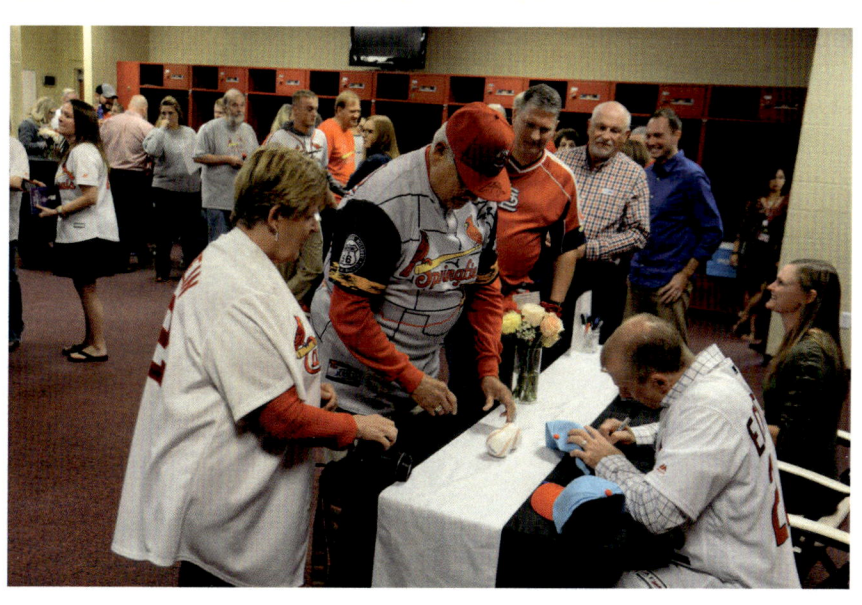

Joanne and Ted Bourbon get an autograph from former Cardinal, David Eckstein, during a "Dinner on the Diamond" post season event.

Walking team photo taken the first week of the 2005 season. The photo was taken for a promotional piece.

This is the first team photo taken of a Springfield Cardinals team. Lots of squinting going on! Notice Pop Warner (middle row far right) with sunglasses.

one. That was a good year to take a team photo because there were a lot of future major league players on that roster, guys like Jaime Garcia, Jon Jay, Chris Perez, Jarrett Hoffpauir, Tyler Greene, Bryan Andersen, Mitchell Boggs, Colby Rasmus, Jason Motte, Matt Pagnozzi, Reed Gorecki, Mike McCoy, and Joe Mather. When I picked our location to take our first team photo, I thought it would look nice to have the team in front of our main gates, which faces west. That was a rookie mistake on my part. The front entrance is concrete with no shade anywhere. It was around 3 p.m. when we finally gathered everyone together for the team shot. The sun was beating down on the players, shining in everyone's eyes. The concrete was radiating heat. The players had their full uniform on which is hot as well. Guys were not complaining too much though. Heck, when I played baseball, I loved it hot. I would wear sleeves in the summer. When I positioned everyone, the last thing to do before taking "keeper shots" is to check my strobe lights. The strobes fill in shadows, making the colors really pop. I snapped a few test shots, feeling satisfied that everything looked great. Mike Lindskog was behind me helping position players. He noticed that our manager, Ron "Pop" Warner, had his sunglasses on. Mike asked Pop to take them off for the photo. Pop ignored the first request. Mike thought he didn't hear him, so he asked again. Warner pushed his glasses down and looked over them and gave Mike a death stare. Warner growled "Ain't gunna happen, Chief." Mike looked at me and we both smiled sheepishly, shrugged our shoulders and proceeded to take shots. Now that I think about it, Pop probably did have a case for being grouchy. Guys were squinting, barely keeping their eyes open. Others just smiled and had no problem with the sun. There were several shots taken. I could tell people were having a difficult time with the sun. I then suggested to everyone, "close your eyes and on the count of three open them." Now there's a little bit of squawking starting up. I could tell I was losing them, so I quickly and loudly counted to three, then took the shot. Pop said, "All right, that's it" so the shoot was over. As each photo opened on my computer, there were three, or four, or five, guys with their eyes closed or squinting badly. Panic was setting in a little bit. Our first team photo, and everyone looked like they were in a chicken rotisserie in a convenience store. I realized too, that I should have had the coaching staff sit in the middle of the front row.

Photoshop has been a go-to friend of mine for years. In a pinch, clone it. One time during a game I was roaming the general admission area out beyond centerfield. A line drive was hit into right center. It looked like an extra base hit. Gorecki dove for it and made a great catch. I was ready and got the shot. At home, the timing of the photo showed the ball in the air about three feet from Gorecki's glove. Reid was completely laid out in mid-air. I thought it would be cool to clone the ball and make it look like it was just about to go into the glove. So, I cloned it. I emailed it to Lindskog. He used it for social media. A day or two later he complimented me on the great photo. I admitted that the ball had been cloned a little closer to the glove than the actual shot. He looked at me like I had robbed a bank. I never did that again.

A team photo is a different story. Every one of these team pictures had at least three or four people with their eyes closed. And it was not always the same players. It took some time, but you can't tell in the photo who had their eyes cloned open, and who had their eyes opened for that shot. There was one fellow that had his eyes closed in

2012 Texas League Championship team guided by Manager Mike Shildt.
Notice that the sun is at their backs? No squinting or complaining!

2017 post team photo having some fun!

every single shot. He ended up with another player's eyes. Can you guess which player it is? Hint: It's not Pop Warner.

The 2012 team photo is hanging on the wall leading to the players lounge. That team is special to me. By now I was a seasoned team photographer and had built great relationships with our players and coaches over the years. This team won the Texas League championship. As of this writing, it is the only championship Springfield has won. There were some great players on that team - Kolten Wong, Trevor Rosenthal, Greg Garcia and the late, great Oscar Taveras among others. Sitting middle front row is current St. Louis manager Mike Shildt. During our 2018 winter caravan, Greg Garcia was one of the traveling players who came to Springfield. He stopped and looked at that photo and you could tell he really enjoyed seeing all those guys he played with. Some made it to the majors while others didn't. Not all players get the break they need to make the big show. Some who don't make it end up staying in baseball as coaches. Top row, second from the end is Chris Swauger. He was a true warrior on the field, has managed in the Cardinals' farm system and in 2019 was named the organization's assistant field coordinator.

If you look closely at the 2012 team photo, you'll notice that the sun is at their backs, and no one is squinting. It seems like this old photographer finally learned something.

CHAPTER 5
ATTRACTING FLIES

Chris Maloney, who is called The Hammer by his players, was our first manager. From the first time I shook his hand I knew he was a genuinely nice guy. He's a southern boy from Mississippi. Chris had that half grin on his face, much like Bruce Willis does in his movies. He played college ball at Mississippi State University from 1983 through 1985. Maloney had a different nickname in college. It's not one a player would covet. Back in college his nickname was "Wally Pipp." Wally Pipp was a 1920's first baseman for the New York Yankees. He was the starting first baseman for the Yankees in 1925 when a rookie by the name of Lou Gehrig made the club for good. Pipp complained about having a headache before a game so manager Miller Huggins substituted Gehrig to replace him. Gehrig went on the play 2,130 consecutive games and poor old Wally Pipp ended up being a footnote in history. Chris had a similar experience. While at MSU, he played first base. Maloney got the stomach flu one day and they put in a young first baseman by the name of Will Clark. Clark went on to major league stardom and was a six time All Star and Gold Glove award winner. Maloney suffered the same fate as Pipp.

Hammer and I clicked from the start. He was always ready to talk baseball with me when we had time before the games. Occasionally I showed up during batting practice, just to watch and talk to whoever might be around, be it a player or coach. Watching those kids take batting practice was making my mouth water. It hadn't been all that long since I had played in men's open leagues around Springfield. During a conversation it was casually brought up that indeed I did play baseball, and a couple years before, was a part-time batting practice pitcher for the Ozark Mountain Ducks. I asked if I could fulfill a bucket list item and shag fly balls during a Cardinals batting practice. Maloney said yes immediately. It was agreed that before the next day's game I could come out and shag. Confidence is something I'm not lacking in. Talent, yes; confidence, no. Well to shag and walk among professional players, It was important to have a professional look while I was out there shagging balls. The last thing I wanted was to look like a fish-out-of-water photographer shagging rockets launched by professional hitters.

My desire was to look like I had been there before, as the old saying goes. The last baseball team I had played for happened to have red uniforms, so red shoes, red belt, and white pants were already taken care of. No purchase required. Hanging in my closet was a solid red shirt undershirt, so that would work. The Cardinals store sold fitted Springfield Cardinal hats. My ensemble was completed with a size seven and a half hat.

Chris told me to arrive about 2:45 if I wanted to stretch with the team before BP. As I walked in, some of the players thought I was a roving minor league coach and didn't realize that it was their team photographer. I broke the ice by making a joke about how your photographer was here to show you how to play the outfield. They laughed and realized it was me. The stretch session was finished so everyone started playing catch - except me. Now I knew how a kid feels when they are the last one picked for a school team. I yelled at our batboy to get his glove so we could play catch. He looked a little surprised but picked up his glove and we started tossing the old horsehide around. The arm was feeling pretty good that day. It was warm, which always helps in loosening up. Then the scoreboard operator cranked up the music like it was a rock concert and batting practice began. When a batter gets in the cage, the first few pitches are supposed to be bunts, then they swing away.

Pitchers and outfielders are the ones who shag in the outfield. Outfielders have priority. Any balls hit in their direction they are to chase down. By working on getting good jumps off the bat during practice, it will translate into a player getting good jumps off the bat during a game. Pitchers on the other hand are there to stand around and talk, catch balls that are hit close to them and act like they care. I decided to stand out in right center field. It was the safest way to stay out of everybody's way. But I wanted to get some action with fly balls too. A few balls were hit my way and I ran them down and made catches. I was loving it. Some of our players came by and said hi and talked while we were waiting for the next line drive. That made me love it even more. I have shagged a lot of fly balls in my life. But when you run down a professional line drive they get to you a whole lot faster. And fly balls are a whole lot higher.

I missed a couple of balls but for the most part it went well. There is a net set up in shallow center field to shield the player collecting balls thrown in from the outfield. A large bucket is behind the net. When the balls are thrown in the player puts them into the bucket. Once the bucket fills up, they take a break, and the player lugs the bucket to the pitcher's mound to dump balls back into the batting practice pitchers' bin. Usually the player gathering balls is the previous game's starting pitcher. Chris Lambert, the

Shagging B.P.

Maloney first gave me permission to shag B.P..

Mike Matheny is greeted by Mike Shildt in a pre-season exhibition game in 2012. Shildt was nice enough to let his photographer shag batting practice balls for a few games.

Chris Lambert ducked just in time when a throw of mine came sailing in unexpectedly.

Seth Maness and Greg Garcia asked how my men's baseball league games were going after coming back to Springfield after making the majors. Manes would stand out in the outfield and chat during bp.

number one draft pick of the Cardinals in 2004, was gathering the balls that day.

When a ball came my way. I caught it, held it up and waited for Chris to look up so I could throw it to him. When you are out there with professional players you want to put all you have into each throw. I didn't want them to think I some weak photographer out there. A line drive was hit to my right. I got a good jump and made a running catch. I looked up at Lambert, held the ball up showing I was getting ready to throw it. He looked right back at me which was my sign to throw it in. I reared back with the intention of throwing a strong, accurate ball, right at his chest. As soon as I fired the ball to Lambert, he turned his head and looked away. Oh no. He had not seen me hold up the ball to let him know I was throwing it to him. The good news is, the throw was strong and accurate. The bad news is, the throw was strong and accurate. My eyes opened in horror as it was sailing towards our 2004 number one draft pick.

I yelled "DUCK CHRIS"! He ducked and dove out of the way at the last second, which is good because it would have surely caught him somewhere on the noggin. I was hoping Chris Maloney had not seen that little excitement. After practice was over, Hammer complimented me on my outfield skills and said I was welcome to come out and shag anytime I wanted to; I didn't even have to ask. It made me feel like he appreciated my love for the game and being around the guys. I did shag several more times that year.

After one session, Matt Gifford, the VP and General Manager, was on the warning track when I was leaving. He had a puzzled look on his face and then asked, "Did you shag balls today?" I downplayed it and acknowledged that I had, that Maloney had invited me. He gave me a look, then said, "Well don't get hurt." I assured him I was careful and always stayed out of the way. If Chris Lambert had not ducked at the last minute, I might have been the first and only team photographer to put a player on the disabled list. It's a pretty safe bet, had he not ducked, I would not be writing this book right now either.

Maloney managed the first two years of Springfield's existence, and then was promoted to Triple A Memphis. I was glad for Hammer, but sad for me. That ushered in the Ron "Pop" Warner era. Pop was all business. He didn't have much time for anyone other than players or coaches. Warner made that clear to me early on, just by the way he handled himself with our staff or fans. There was no way I would ask for permission to shag balls. He managed Springfield for five years, which is a very long time to manage the same team in minor league baseball. I had very few conversations with him in those five years that lasted more than a minute. Eventually Pop was promoted to manage in Memphis. That vacancy was filled by a person not well known by Cardinals fans, but highly regarded by management. Named to manager the Springfield Cardinals for 2012 was Mike Shildt. He was a true southern gentleman. A baseball lifer. Mike's mother's name is Lib. She had worked for the Baltimore Orioles minor league team in Charlotte, N.C. Mike was a batboy and filled some other jobs too. When I got to know Mike a little better, I mentioned that Maloney had let me shag from time to time. Shildt invited me to come out and shag. Of course, I accepted. My confidence level in doing quality batting practice shagging was now a little suspect. It had been five years since Maloney let me do it. There were no recent men's league games to keep sharp. I was now 56 years old. Let's face it, I was rusty to say the least. But I would not have hinted that I wanted to do it if I didn't feel like I was still capable. After all, I do love challenges. Plus, Gifford instructed me not to get hurt so there was that added pressure.

Out of storage came the same spikes, pants, belt and shirt. For some reason the pants were a little tighter and the belt needed adjusting but I just figured it was because they were getting older and shrunk while in storage.

The 2012 team was filled with great ballplayers who were also very nice. When I trotted out to the outfield to assume my place in right center, they were very welcoming. The pitchers were more than happy to let me get anything I could reach. This team could hit too. Oscar Taveras, Kolten Wong, Greg Garcia, Xavier Scruggs and Jermaine Curtis could all put a charge in the baseball. I think the hardest ball I ever caught was off the bat of Kolten Wong. He hit one on the button right at me and it got to me in a hurry. It almost tore my glove off, but I held onto it. It was a fun team, and a winning team. Not only did it have hitting and defense, it had some amazing pitching. My shagging career came to an end when Shildt left after three seasons. I knew it was time to hang up the spikes before I got hurt. It was a good run while it lasted.

CHAPTER 6
EVOLUTION OF THE DUGOUT

Selecting places to sit and shoot during a game used to be more of a challenge than it is now. From Maloney through Warner, the closest I ever got to the dugout during the game was in the photographers well. If the crowd isn't all that big, it opens up the opportunity to move around and get different angles by sitting in empty seats in the stadium. It allows you to get closer to position players too. It's always tough to get action shots of the outfielders because of the distance. A $15,000 lens would be nice to get for far off shots, but my budget does not allow for that. During a typical evening game, after pre-game, I will start out in the third base well. That angle puts the sun to my back. In early spring or late summer games, shadows from the third base side creep onto the infield right when the game starts. That limits taking quality photos until the sun goes down and the lights take full effect. I will have one inning to get our starting pitcher in sunshine. The shadows move across the infield which can provide a harsh contrast between dark shadows and bright sunlight. That is tricky lighting. From May through July, I have a lot more sun to work with, which is always welcomed.

In the third base well, occasionally I will have a visiting player come by during the game and start up a conversation. One of the more memorable moments in third base well history came during a game against Northwest Arkansas. Vance Wilson, the manager, was a real firebrand. He had eight years of major league experience as a back-up catcher for the Tigers and Mets. He probably had the shortest fuse of all managers who have managed a game at Hammons. Vance was always nice to me, shaking hands and asking how I was doing. The Naturals had Terrance Gore on their team, a real speed demon. At that time, he was one of the fastest men in all of baseball. He could run like the wind, which is what he hit most of the time when he swung a bat. He never hit much in the minors, but he was such a fast runner that the Royals brought him up in 2014 to pinch run during the playoffs and World Series. In 16 career major league at bats, he was 1 for 16, with 27 stolen bases in 31 attempts. Leading off the game this day, Gore chopped a ball down the third base line, and was off to the races. My camera was ready for the play at first. It was a close call, but the umpire called him out. In my mind, he had beaten the throw. Running from the third base coaching box, Wilson was screaming and yelling at the umpire. His veins were popping out, his eyes were on fire and his language, let's just say, was creative. Those type of arguments are somewhat rare in my time with the Cardinals. Wilson was the best at getting fired up during an argument. Brian Poldberg, the Naturals manager before Wilson, was a close second for getting in an umpire's face. None of the Springfield Cardinals managers were animated like Vance. I would jokingly ask umpires before a game if they could blow a call so I could get some good argument shots. The umps always laughed.

After a minute or two, it was inevitable that Wilson would get tossed from the game. Gore came trotting back to their dugout, ready to simmer on the bench. As Wilson was making his way into the visitor's clubhouse, I began scrolling through the sequence of shots. It clearly showed that Gore was safe. Terrance saw me looking at the camera preview, so he came over and asked if I got the shot. I shook my head yes, then held the camera up, zooming in on his foot. The photo clearly showed his foot on the base before the ball arrived to first. He jumped and said, "I knew it!". He walked back and sat on the bench. My mind started running through all the things that could happen if Gore told Wilson that the umps had blown the call. If Gore told Wilson after the game that the Cardinals photographer had proof that he safe, Vance would be able to bring it up to the umpires the following day. My mind started wondering as to what might happen the next day during pre-game when the umpires and managers exchange line-up cards at home plate. I could envision me running by home plate, ready to position our field of dream kids. As I passed home plate, Wilson could call me over to show the umpires the shot of them missing the call at first base. Gulp! After pondering all that could go wrong, I motioned Gore to come over to talk with me. He had a puzzled look on his face and walked over. I said "Terrance, please keep your safe-at-first photograph secret, and don't tell Wilson I have it. I don't want Vance to tell the umpires that the Cardinals photographer showed you the shot that proved they blew the call." He laughed and then said, "Knowing Wilson, that's probably a good idea. I won't tell." It taught me a lesson to never show a player a photo of a close play again, unless the umpire was correct on the call.

In the course of a season it's easy to get locked into gravitating towards a few go-to spots to shoot. It's nice to mix it up once every so often. Once during a morning game, I climbed onto the roof of the main office and took some shots from there. The only way to get up there was by way of a ladder. It was awkward trying to climb up the stairs, one hand over the other, with my camera dangling around my neck. Once I arrived at the top of the roof, I was amazed at how many baseballs were up there. There were dozens of balls that had either been home runs during a game or batting practice homers. A few times I have climbed to the top of our manual scoreboard in left field to get a different perspective. You have to climb up a ladder to a deck, then take another ladder to the top of the scoreboard. When you shoot from up there is looks like a drone shot.

For years I had wanted to shoot a game in the Cardinals dugout, but I didn't want to be in their way. When we played St. Louis in exhibition games, I noticed that their photographer had shot in the St. Louis dugout, and made a mental note. The dugout is truly a place where I can get shots no one else can get - up close and personal. While chatting with an umpire during pre-game, I asked if there was a rule against a team photographer being in the dugout. He said no, as long as it is OK with the manager. This was good information that could be useful down the road. During Maloney's time, I was too new to have the guts to ask. During Warner's time as manager, I was too intimidated to ask. When Shildt came to Springfield, he really upped my confidence as a photographer and made me feel like I was part of the team. I had never asked him if I could shoot in the dugout, but it was always in the back of my mind. My dugout world changed forever when Yadier Molina came to Springfield on a two-game rehabilitation assignment. It was such a special moment because Greg Garcia also was back in town on a rehab assignment. Michael Wacha was in town for a rehab start as well. To put icing on the cake, Willie McGee was in town as a roving instructor. Now that's a pretty big game with all those St. Louis players here at once.

Clockwise: Yadi Molina, Michael Wacha, and Willie McGee were in town for the first game I ever photographed in the Springfield dugout. Middle left: My hunting chair keeps me safely behind the netting.

Just before the game started, I was sort of leaning over the well trying to get good dugout shots. Mike saw me leaning and signaled me over. I jumped the netting and went into the dugout. He said, "You should shoot the game from our dugout. This will be a great game for that." The umpires had cleared the way for me a couple years before, answering my questions about the rules, and Shildt just completed my bucket list by giving me his approval to be in the dugout for the first time. What a first game it was. The game was sold out. Everybody came to see Yadi. As I knelt behind the netting for protection, someone tapped me on my shoulder. It was Willie McGee. He invited me to stand next to him, which was a much better spot to be than where I was, behind a pole next to the trash can. Gee, thanks Willie, I said. As I scanned my new location, I realized I was standing between McGee and Wacha, with Yadi directly behind me putting on his catcher's gear. Now that is what I'm talking about - dugout baseball. Shots from the dugout are so much better. You can shoot lower to the ground. You can position yourself for double plays at second. And the candid shots are endless, whether it's a guy getting high fives after a home run, or a pitcher who's been taken out of the game and is sitting dejected on the bench. Being in the dugout has a huge responsibility attached to it. Always be sure not to get in anybody's way. Don't bug players or coaches. Don't give your opinion as to what coaching move to make. Don't yell at an opposing player or umpire. And most importantly, never take your eye off the ball when it's pitched. Foul balls scream into the dugout from time to time.

I have a small hunting seat I keep in the home photographers well. When I am going into the dugout, the seat goes with me. It unfolds to a height of about two feet.

48

Just by sitting on it, my eyes are the perfect height to shoot great shots, while being protected by the dugout netting. I am probably the safest person in there. I've had a few close calls with foul balls while sitting in the stands, but never one in the dugout.

CHAPTER 7
CLOSE ENCOUNTERS OF THE FOUL BALL KIND

There have been some close calls for me concerning foul balls. When Hammons Field was newly opened for business, fans loved it because they were up close to the action, much closer than in major league stadiums. There can be a problem with being close to the action, however. If a hitter is late on his swing, the ball can slice right into the crowd in a millisecond, sometimes causing serious injury. A few times a year you will see a bat slip out of a hitter's hand on his back swing and the bat will fly into the stands. Obviously, that can be a dangerous situation. In 2016 Springfield management decided to make changes to their netting layout to make it safer for fans. The original netting went from the on-deck circle to the visiting team's on-deck circle, which left an unprotected gap from the on-deck circle all the way down both foul lines. Foul balls hit straight back over the netting would crash into the concourse. In 2016 netting was extended from the far end of one dugout and wrapped all the way to the far end of the other dugout. It's 8 feet higher and 100 feet wider down both sides of the field after the changes were implemented. The new netting took away some of my short cuts to the field, but it was a trade-off I happily accepted for the sake of safety.

Here's a funny story about foul balls. In the minor leagues, American League minor league affiliates play against National League affiliates, which raises the question, "What do you do with the designated hitter rule?" When the Cardinals play a fellow National League affiliated team, the designated hitter rule goes out the window. Pitchers for the most part love to hit so this is their time to get in some swings. This story happened in 2013, in a game against the Tulsa Drillers, which at that time was the affiliate of the Colorado Rockies. The Rockies are a National League club, meaning there would be no designated hitter.

Around the seventh inning left handed reliever Justin Wright was scheduled to bat. Relievers rarely get to bat as they usually get pinch hit for when their time to bat comes up. But this time, he went up to the plate to take a few swings. Although he throws left handed, Wright batted right handed. On the first pitch he swung late and hit a laser beam foul right into the Cardinals dugout, scattering a few guys. Before the next pitch everybody went back to their spot on the bench. The next pitch produced another late swing by Justin. This time he hit outfielder Adam Melker right in the butt. Apparently, Wright was not able to get around on the other pitcher's fastball. Justin stepped out of the batter's box and started giggling after he hit Melker. Now our guys were starting to pay attention to Wright at the plate. There were also a few hitting tips being yelled his way too. The third pitch came sizzling in and Wright was late on the swing again. The foul ball went bouncing around the dugout like it was in a pinball machine. Justin stepped out of the box again, trying to contain his laughter.

Before the next pitch everybody in the dugout started kneeling behind the concrete retaining wall with netting along the railing. They looked like World War 1 soldier's, peeking over the edge of the trench into no-man's-land. Not too surprisingly, Justin struck out on the next pitch when the pitcher decided to put an end to Wright's amusement by throwing him a nasty breaking ball for a called third strike. Wright started slowly walking back to the dugout with his bat in hand, staring at the ground with a grin. When he looked up, some of the guys were standing on the dugout steps waiving white towels in a sign of surrender. He broke out into a laugh. Some fans started laughing and clapping for their lefty reliever who provided some unexpected entertainment.

The closest I've ever come to being struck by a foul ball was when Joe Mather played for us. He was moving up the ladder fast to the big leagues. Joe was tall, good looking, personable, and a fun guy. The ladies loved him. Joe's agent had contacted me, requesting a photo to be used on a Topps baseball card featuring top prospects. Having my photos appear on baseball cards has always been a treat for me. The only thing I would have liked better would be ME on a baseball card as a player. My plan was to get a good shot of Joe in the first inning, when the sun was still in a good spot for taking photos of batters. After the first inning, the shadows crept over home plate and it was not the kind of light you want for a baseball card. There were several shots that were good enough for a card that had already been taken but having one of him in full swing, watching the flight of the ball is what I wanted. To get a righthanded hitter's follow through swing from third base requires waiting until the bat has gone through the hitting zone and is about to be let go by the top hand. It's dangerous for a photographer to shoot that shot from third base if they don't have a protective net in front of them. The wells do have netting, but you must get down on both knees to stoop low enough. If you don't have long pants on, the rough concrete makes it a little uncomfortable on the knees. This day I happened to be wearing shorts. To get the shot I wanted, I had to focus on the batter and keep shooting until the swing was finished. If a ball is hit right at the photographer, they really don't know if it is coming at them or not, because their eye is up against the view finder. Playing as much baseball as I have, waiting for that shot without knowing where the ball is, it not smart. Yet, I wanted a great shot for a Joe's prospect Topps card, so I told myself that the odds of Joe hitting a ball at me were small.

In the well there was some trash and wet sandbags, making it very unpleasant to kneel behind the netting for protection. My camera was trained on Mather when he stepped to the plate. If the pitcher didn't give Joe a pitch to hit, then I would not get the shot that night because the sun would not be where I needed it to be. Nothing is more frustrating than to need a shot of a batter only to have him get a base on balls or look foolish on a swing against a good breaking ball.

Mather stepped into the batter's box, waving his bat around, looking for a good pitch to hit. It didn't take long. Joe swung at the first pitch and connected. My five frames per second mode was set, so just keeping my finger on the button kept the camera shooting throughout the swing. Mather had a nice swing at an inside fastball. He hit it right on the button. But I noticed he was looking towards me, following the ball. My instinct told me to duck as quickly as I could because there was a good chance a foul ball was coming my way. Right in the middle of my bailing out, I felt a slight burn on my neck, like somebody pulled my hair. Then there was a loud rattling sound in the dugout, which sounded a lot like a baseball. The ball never hit me, only grazed me. The crowd had made a collective gasp when they saw the foul ball buzz by me. Many assumed I had

Foul Ball Stories

Justin Wright's late swing causes players to duck and cover in the dugout.

Joe Mather watching his line drive foul ball head straight for my camera (and my head).

been hit, including Mike Lindskog, who told his radio audience that Mark, our team photographer had been hit by the ball. It rolled by my feet. After making sure I was all in one piece, I stood up and waved to the crowd, affirming that I was indeed safe and unhurt. There was a laugh and cheer. A young fan leaned over and asked if he could have the ball, so I tossed it to him. Many times, I have regretted not saving that ball. I should have had Joe sign it for me. It was the ball that almost killed me, or at the least gave me some bruises for a few days. Fortunately for me, I got a perfect shot, baseball card worthy. That night I decided to print out the best photo of the sequence, have Joe sign it, and hang in my office. Rarely do I ask for autographs, but this was a memory I wanted to keep.

At the game the following night, Joe Mather was nowhere to be found. I looked around and finally asked one of the coaches where Mather was. He said that Joe had been promoted to Memphis and was leaving that night. The photo was in my bag and it looked like I would miss this opportunity to get it signed. Down the right field line, I saw a tall young man walking in street clothes. It turned out it was Joe. As I approached him, he said, "I thought I killed you with my foul ball last night." I said, "Yeah, you and the rest of the ballpark." Mather's photo came out of my bag along with a sharpie. He looked at it and wrote the following: "To Mark, have you seen my baseball? Joe Mather."

CHAPTER 8
WORLD SERIES BONUS (SORT OF)

With the last out of the 2013 World Series, my hope for a World Series bonus went out the window. While I am not actually eligible for a World Series bonus, I get an indirect bonus of sorts if the Cardinals win. Let me explain. The Cardinals won the series in 2006. The first Springfield Cardinal to ever appear in a World Series was former Springfield closer Josh Kinney. He came through with some great relief appearances. Josh came from obscurity, pitching for the River City Rascals, an independent Frontier League team, before he signed with the Cardinals organization. He worked his way up and became an important part of the bullpen, working 1 1/3 shutout innings in the World Series. He contributed to the Cardinals victory over the Detroit Tigers. When Adam Wainwright struck out Brandon Inge to end the World Series, little did I know that I would be receiving an indirect bonus in April of 2007.

Most of the time when a person gets a bonus, it's handed to you in the form of a check. Not mine. It was delayed a bit too, and totally unexpected. In addition, I had to work my rear end off for this bonus. As the 2007 season got under way, it was announced that last year's 2006 World Series Trophy would be traveling from Busch Stadium to Hammons Field. Matt Gifford, armed with his white kid gloves, went to St Louis to pick up the trophy and bring it back to Springfield. The trophy was on loan to the team for three days. The idea of the trophy coming to town was exciting. Gifford told me of the plan to have fans form a line and pose with the trophy for pictures. The fans would just take the photos with their own camera or cellphone.

He thought for a minute and said, "If you want to set up your strobe lights and take shots for the fans and sell them online, that would be fine with me." It sounded like a pretty good idea to me. On the first day, the trophy was set up along the upper area just beyond the right field seats. above the Cardinals bullpen area. Management thought there would be plenty of room for people to form a line, pose with the trophy and move on. We really didn't know how many people to expect.

Earlier in the day, we had set up a backdrop with Cardinals logos scattered all over the front. A table was placed in front of the backdrop and then the trophy was laced in the middle of the table. The setup was completed in time for an appreciation luncheon for our sponsors. After lunch, everyone was welcome to pose with the trophy. Matt had asked if I would attend the luncheon to get shots of our sponsors, which I gladly did. Little did I know that those photos were just a drop in the bucket for was what to come. The evening came, the gates opened, and a flood of fans wanted their picture with the trophy. The line started snaking all the way down the stairs, wrapping around the outside right field fence. The only thing to do was to roll up my sleeves and start taking photos as fast as I could. There was a sign by the trophy that said NO TOUCHING of the trophy. A Greene County deputy sheriff was assigned the task of making sure everyone obeyed the rules. My routine was to let them quickly take a picture with their phone or camera if they wanted and then I took a nice one with strobe lights. We hurried as quickly as possible because the line was so long. If there is a world record for saying "ready, 1, 2, 3, smile," I probably would have broken it that night. It was amazing. Thank goodness my strobe lights held out. I had no idea it would be that busy. I took more than 700 photos that night, and we still had two more games to show off the trophy.

The next night it rained, and the wind was blowing hard. We decided to set up the Springfield Cardinals backdrop, and my lights, in the team store. There was not enough room, but we made do with what we had. We pulled off some great crowd management and shot all evening until everyone had gone through that wanted a picture. There were probably more people that went through the team store in that one evening than the entire season. It is easy to get fatigued when you're saying "1, 2, 3, smile" all night. Just because you take the photo does not mean the job is done. They still need to be cropped and uploaded to my website. I burned the midnight oil both nights to get them posted. From experience, I was aware how impatient fans become. I knew they would start asking when the photos were going to be online. The morning of day three of our trophy fest, I decided to call my old buddy Ned Reynolds. He was the host of "The Sports Reporters" a morning radio sports talk show. My purpose was to let people know the status of the trophy photos. I wanted them to understand that it takes some time and not to be nervous. I would have them online in a day or two. Right on que, I had been getting emails asking why the photos were not online yet. My initial reaction was, "Did you not see the amount of people who went through that line?" But I thought I could save some potential email inquiries if I told Ned's listening audience to please be patient, that it might take a couple of days to get them online. He was gracious to let me go on the show.

The third day was just as busy. During the three days, I took more than 3,000 photos of people standing by that trophy. As I started posting the photos, people started complaining that they had to search through all the photos to find theirs. There was only one photo album per day, each one with several hundred photos. The problem was, I had not thought out the cataloging and organizing process enough. There was no way to have known there would be that sort of volume. Orders started flooding in. When an order came in, I received an email confirmation, showing each order. Signing into my email the next few mornings was like hitting the jackpot on a slot machine. My email inbox was swamped. People were buying all sizes and quantities.

My next opportunity for an indirect World Series bonus came because of the Cardinals' improbable win in the 2011 World Series. During the historic game six (the David Freese game) I had my hand on the remote, ready to shut off the television when the Cardinals were one strike away from defeat. I am not a good loser and the last thing I wanted was to watch the Texas Rangers celebrate. Freese sure came through not only once, but twice, that night to extend the Series to game seven, which turned out to be a Red Bird winner. When Jason Motte got the last out, I jumped up and cheered for two reasons. Of course, I was happy that the Cardinals had won an incredibly suspenseful World Series. The other reason was the trophy would be coming to Springfield for a visit. This time when the trophy came to Hammons, we were all ready. We set up the Cardinals backdrop in the indoor batting cage facility, taking any sort of weather problem out of the equation, which includes a gust of wind knocking down my lights or backdrop. Gates opened two hours before the games to give fans more of a chance to get their picture taken. Gifford had assigned an assistant for me, helping

2011 World Series Trophy in Springfield

Top: Louie with Trophy

Middle: Dan Reiter shows off the artwork on bottom of Trophy

Bottom: 2012 stadium crew

move the line along, and taking cell phone pictures for those who wanted one. It made for a long but productive three days. Another lesson learned from 2006 was to save the photos in an album, by the date, and the hour it was taken. Fans would no longer have to scroll through hundreds of photos to find theirs on my website. They could find them within the time frame when they went through the line.

The trophy photos turned into such an event that two television stations came out to shoot some live footage of the crowd. Both stations wanted to interview me during the middle of my photo shoot, and I was more than happy to do so. Just like with the 2006 trophy, I took more than 3,000 photos over those three days. My internet orders came flowing in which meant my indirect World Series bonus was once again paying off. The Cardinals were World Series bound once again in 2013. We went storming through the playoffs and into the series, but the bats got cold against a Boston team that was hotter than a St Louis doubleheader in August. This series was almost surreal for me. Half the team played for Springfield at one time or another and I was friends with them. In 2006, I knew one player. We didn't win the series that year and I didn't get an indirect bonus. But one of the nice things about being part of St Louis Cardinal baseball is knowing you have a decent chance almost every year to go to the big show. Not many teams can say that.

CHAPTER 9
THREE NIGHTS OF RADIO

Earlier I had mentioned that back in my Ozark Mountain Duck independent baseball days, I provided color, and play-by-play from time to time, on the radio broadcasts. Team photographer was also on my plate. Those were some of the most fun times I have ever had at a baseball game, playing or otherwise. I've saved several old cassette tapes of games I called during that period. Opening a drawer one day I came upon some of the tapes. I popped in a couple into a recorder to see what they sounded like. As I was listening, I thought to myself "You know, that ain't half bad." I am my worst critic, so for me not to cringe while listening to the tape was a good sign. Since I started working with Springfield, the person I take orders from is the Broadcaster & Public Relations Manager. It's important to have a good relationship with whomever is in that position. Mike Lindskog was our first, followed by Jeff Levering, and currently serving in that capacity is Andrew Buchbinder. Each one was kind enough to let me be a guest during a broadcast or two. The reason was always to promote our photo website. I was relaxed in the booth and tried to make it lighthearted and fun for whoever was interviewing me. Back in the early days of the Springfield Cardinals when Mike Lindskog was the voice of the team, he told me if I ever wanted to go on the road and do color, I would be welcome. I couldn't ever muster up enough courage to take him up on his generous offer - not because I wasn't confident about being able to do it, but I wasn't sure how well Gifford would take it. I was very confident that I could do a good job, but I didn't want to take any chances that if I did mess up, it might jeopardize my team photographer status

When Mike left, Jeff Levering replaced him. Jeff is a great guy, with a great voice, and a good baseball intellect. He is currently serving as the television play-by-play announcer for the Milwaukee Brewers. He gets to work with Bob Uecker, which has got to be a blast. Jeff knew that I knew baseball pretty well so when I felt the time was right, I threw out the fact I had radio experience broadcasting baseball games. Once again, he told me that any time I wanted to go on the road to call a game, I was invited. The temptation was getting greater and greater, but I still had not gotten up the nerve. My chance with Jeff passed when he accepted a job with the Boston Red Sox Triple A Pawtucket team. When we lose a Broadcaster & Public Relations Manager, it's always important to get to know the new person because we work closely on projects such as portraits, team photos, action shots, baseball card photos and more. Management selected a young fellow by the name of Andrew Buchbinder to replace Levering. He had been the play by play man for the Hickory Crawdads of the South Atlantic League. The Crawdads are an affiliate of the Texas Rangers. Andrew could not be more pleasant and is a genuinely nice guy. He came up to my studio to have his publicity head shot taken right before the first game in 2013. I gave him my take on things that he should know about Springfield, some of the fans and the personalities of the staff and a general history of Springfield. He appreciated it and we started working on getting ready for opening day. We set up a time for player portraits and just like that the season started. Once I got to know Andrew, I mentioned that I used to do radio play-by-play and wondered if I might travel on the road sometime with him and do color on the broadcasts. I figured now would be the time. He said that he had no problem at all with that. The reason road games are more of an option for me is because Andrew has a booth partner for home games, and I am busy taking photos. On the road he was by himself. It's nice to be able to bounce things off another person during a game and get their perspective. As the summer wore on, the desire to call a game finally got the best of me. It was mid-season and the Cardinals were traveling to Springdale, Ark., to play the Naturals, the Kansas City Royals affiliate. It was only a two-hour drive and I knew the area well. On the second to last game of our homestand I went up to the radio booth and pitched the idea to Andrew. "Would you mind if I called a game with you this weekend?" I asked. He said yes. I suggested that we should get it cleared first with Gifford. I had visions of Matt driving his car, tuning into the Naturals game and hearing me, not knowing that I would be on the radio. It might have caused him to lose control of his automobile. Andrew thought that was a good idea, so he got the go ahead from Matt. That made me feel much better. Gifford had suggested to Andrew that I should not come on until the third inning to give fans a chance to settle in. That was cool with me.

The drive to Arkansas was a blur. I'm sure people who passed me on the highway were wondering why I was enthusiastically talking to myself. I had not lost my marbles but was practicing and exercising my voice for the game. I rolled into Springdale about three hours before the game so I could get my bearings. I was also hopeful that I might be able to stand around the batting cage during batting practice and pick up some tidbits for the broadcast. After all, I knew all the players and coaches. Buchbinder had arranged for my press pass to be waiting for me at will call. I picked it up and was feeling giddy by that time. An usher pointed out the visitor's radio booth a I climbed the stairs and found Buchbinder already preparing for the game. He gave me all sorts of stats along with a website to get even more information. The most important thing to learn in pre-game preparation is how to pronounce names. There are some very tricky ones. When I did games for the Ducks, some of the opposing players were from Japan. Their names looked like Egyptian hieroglyphics to me. I wrote them phonetically instead of the actual spelling. My iPad was along for the ride to help me look up stats as the game went along. I was able to go online and get enough useless information to sound like a real authority. It took me about half of a game to realize that is not my style.

The Cardinals were taking the field for batting practice, so I decided to take a short trip down to see if anyone would talk with me. As I walked on the field several players came over to me with a surprised look, asking what I was doing there. I told them I was doing color on the radio, so they had better be nice to me. Stephen Piscotty was nice enough to give me insight into how he was feeling and what his game plan might be. The guys thought that was cool that I had made the trip. I asked a few general questions to the fellas. When they answered the question, they went into detail, just like Jack Buck had asked them. Mike Shildt came over and said, "So tonight's the night huh?" I laughed and said yes, no turning back now. I commented, "well since you're here, give me some thoughts into how you are going approach tonight's game." Mike, being Mike, started sharing his plan for the night, who was available to pitch, and other bits of information that might come in handy for me to use during the broadcast. I can't tell you how much that meant to me that Shildty took the time out during batting practice to chat. The same went for coaches Randy Nieman and Phil Wellman. Both gave me a few minutes and made me feel like a real radio guy.

Back up to the booth I went, walking on clouds. The weird thing was, I was never nervous, just excited. Andrew and I enjoyed the press box food provided by the Naturals. We went back to the booth and prepared for the game. I sat patiently waiting for the third inning so I could jump in. While Andrew called the first two innings, I was looking up stats and making notes so I could be the next Tim McCarver. Finally, Andrew introduced me in the top of the third, and we were rolling. As a play unfolded, I put in my two cents after Andrew finished his thoughts about the play. I missed a few plays because I was busy looking up stats, so I could mention them at the right time. About the sixth inning a bell went off in my head. I told myself "Push those stats to the side and start trusting yourself." After the inning ended and we went to break I told Andrew, "Man you are awesome at pointing out inside stats, I am leaving that up to you and I'm just going to start observing and fly from the seat of my pants." He chuckled and said I was doing great.

The game was fun because it featured the debut of the Kansas City Royals top pitching prospect, Kyle Zimmer. He dominated the Cardinals and recorded his first win. It was fun in the booth because I was getting texts from family and friends during the game commenting and telling me I was doing a good job (what else would they say?). That was new for me because there was no texting, or for that matter iPads available, in my Mountain Ducks days. Andrew included me in the post-game wrap up and I now had my first Cardinals game under my belt. Buchbinder

Radio Play by Play

Andrew Buchbinder has been our Broadcaster & Public Relations Manager since the 2013 season. Andrew allowed me to be his "color commentator" for three road games in 2013.

Former Baltimore Orioles great and MLB Hall of Famer Jim Palmer visited Hammons Field to promote the Cystic Fibrosis Foundation. Lindskog is shaking hands while broadcaster Rob Evans looks on.

Mike Lindskog was paid a visit by a "Praying Mantis" up in the radio booth. Lindskog had a giant iguana as a house pet. I wonder if this uninvited visitor ended up being a post-game meal.

Springfield business owner Marty Prather, sends a light hearted message to Cardinals Hitting Instructor Phil Wellman. Bottom (R) Prather recycles sign for Wellman, who later managed the San Antonio Missions. Marty has been featured in national publications, newspapers, and television, highlighting his clever use of signage at sporting events.

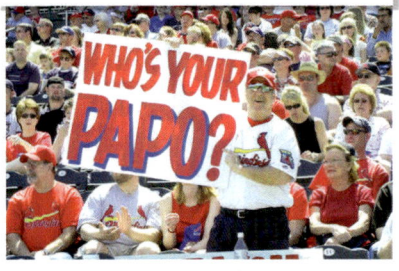

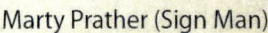

Marty Prather (Sign Man)

thanked me and said he really appreciated me being there, knowing well how hard it is to call a game by yourself. I said "Well, so it's good for me to call the game tomorrow as well?" He said "Absolutely, would love to have you back tomorrow." I went back to the hotel walking on air. I tossed and turned in bed that night replaying the game in my head. I finally fell to sleep excited for tomorrow's game.

The next day I was at the ballpark early again. Shildty told me that his mom Lib listened to the game online and really enjoyed it. That was music to my ears. Then Philip Wellman our hitting coach came up to me and said he'd heard some of the game in the locker room and he thought I did a nice job. Sweet praise coming from him. When Wellman first came to Springfield all the talk was about him centered on how much of an internet sensation he was. His tirade while managing the Mississippi Braves is one for the ages. In March 2009, ESPN showed the top-10 meltdowns in sports history and judged Wellman's to be the number 1 meltdown. If you want to see it, I'm sure you can find it on YouTube. As a result of that, Phil was selected to play himself in a Volkswagen commercial broadcast during the Super Bowl, along with several other people who had melt-downs in the spotlight. He looks like a bouncer getting ready to throw you out of a bar. But in reality; he's one of the nicest, Christian men you will ever meet.

I went through the same routine as the previous night and spent time around the batting cages gathering inside information that I might use. I was amazed at how that information had come in handy during the previous night's game. Before the game Andrew said, "Why don't you come in during our pre-game and talk about last night's game?" Then he added, "There's no need to wait until the third inning, let's get you in from the start." That gave me a sense of comfort knowing that Buchbinder wanted me on the air with him from the git-go. The first game gave me confidence for this upcoming one. It went well even though the Cardinals lost. Andrew said he appreciated my inside baseball knowledge and that it made his job easier.

He was sincere in his comments and I left Arkansas with a new respect for Andrew. He was so prepared and knowledgeable. He made it look easy. It is NOT easy. The Cardinals went on an eight-day road trip so by the time they got back to Springfield I had come down to Earth and was ready to assume my job as team photographer. A few fans over the next few games told me they enjoyed my radio appearance. I was very flattered. The cherry on top was when Matt Gifford walked by during our pre-game ceremony and said, "Hello radio star." I was able to get one more game in as a guest color commentator. I took a trip to Tulsa to call one game. The Cardinals were in a pennant race for the Northern Division's second half championship so there was something riding on the game. Other than a home-made scorecard and the roster in front of me, I added my two cents in when I felt it was appropriate. Andrew was a fabulous host and I thought we had nice chemistry. I threw out some humor and he played right along with it. Check this one off on my bucket list.

CHAPTER 10
SWEET DREAMS

When I have a camera around my neck and I'm running around Hammons Field shooting photos, I usually have some adrenalin flowing – at least most of the time. This story begins with me going through the day with a pounding headache. Tylenol is always my go-to pain reliever, so I popped a couple pills in my mouth, downed some water and headed for the game. Pre-game is always a little stressful because there are several things that need to be done in a certain time frame, including first pitches and the Field of Dreams Kids. After getting pre-game out of the way, which is always the priority, I headed for the photographers well to begin my nightly trek going from well to well, and everywhere in between. After jumping into the first base well it occurred to me that my head was not throbbing like it had been, which was nice. Staring into the sun while it is disappearing over the stands certainly doesn't help a headache, but it looked like that would not be an issue. As the action was going on and the photos were being taken, I started relaxing to the point of yawning. That doesn't happen often because of the fast nature of the job. In pointing the camera at my subject, my finger just sat there. I was watching the action but didn't care if I took a shot or not. All I wanted to do was take a nap. The thought occurred to me that I might be coming down with an illness. Changing locations and getting my blood flowing might do the trick.

Moving to the third base well would do that trick. As I was changing the lens on my camera, there was a vision that popped into my head. It was my bathroom sink. Next to the sink was a bottle of Tylenol. The same bottle I used to get rid of my headache. Then it occurred to me, that I had taken two Tylenol PM. That is a large dose for somebody wanting to stay awake. It was the second inning so there was plenty of game left. If I was going to function at all I had no option other than going to my car and taking a 20-minute power nap. I don't remember much about the walk to my car, but somehow, I got there. After getting into my car and cracking the windows a bit for fresh air, I was ready for my twenty-minute power nap. It didn't take long to dose off.

About two hours later, someone had hit a home run, which caused a roar from the crowd. The sound carried all the way out to the west parking lot woke me up. Peeking through bleary eyes to find the car radio, I tuned in to see what inning the game was in. It was the bottom of the eighth. I shook my head, turned on the car and drove home, wondering to myself if I should tell anybody what a dumb thing I had just done. What the heck, if you can't have a sense of humor and laugh at yourself, then a person is just too serious.

CHAPTER 11
HEAD OVER HEELS

Luke Voit played for Springfield during the 2016 season. He's from Wildwood, Mo, a suburb of St. Louis and attended Missouri State University in Springfield. Voit was an important part of the MSU Bears baseball program, anchoring down catching duties during his time there. The Bears share Hammons Field with the Cardinals, so Luke was very familiar with the Springfield facility when he joined the team. That is, he was familiar with the catcher's position. When he signed with St. Louis, he was converted to a first baseman. He took to the new position and showed continuous improvement around the bag. He had a great season, becoming a Texas League All Star as well as winning the All-Star home run derby contest. Voit electrified the hometown crowd with one bomb after another. His hat was turned backwards just like Ken Griffey Jr. use to do. While getting action shots of the derby, I roamed around the outfield while the show was in progress. Kids were shagging balls and we all got to see what some of those moon shots looked like from an outfielder's perspective. Hammons has hitter-friendly dimensions, with left field measuring 315 down the line. After the month of April there is usually a nice breeze blowing out towards left field. But those derby participants didn't need any help. Luke received a fancy hunting knife from Bass Pro Shops and a trophy for winning the event. When Buchbinder awarded Luke the prize, he took the knife out of the holder and stabbed up at the sky, yelling something along the likes of "SHABAAZZ". He had been yelling that all season every time something good happened on the field. I wondered what in the world that meant; it was driving me crazy, so I had to ask him, what the phrase meant that he had been screaming all year? He laughed and said it was from the movie "Dirty Grandpa" which was way out of my age demographic for comedy appreciation.

He made a defensive play at first base in one game that ended up being a frequently played scoreboard video highlight before games. It all started with a high foul pop up drifting towards the Cardinals dugout. Voit bolted from his position heading straight for the dugout. You could hear his footsteps getting closer and closer in pursuit of the foul ball. It sounded like a freight train roaring down the tracks as I watched him from the dugout steps. The trash can was to my right. If the wind is just right, the smell from the trash can will waft over into the bench area. While looking up to see if I could tell where the ball might end up, it occurred to me that I was in the landing zone. Luke might fall on me, but I was more concerned about my camera. I was backing up from the trash can area because I wanted no part of that foul ball. When a ball hits concrete it sounds like a mortar round landing. Luke was lumbering after that foul ball and had a look in his eyes that said, "I'm going to catch this even if I have to run through the railing." As he started drifting closer to the dugout, my instincts to take a photo was overtaken by my instinct to survive without Voit and his 225 pounds tumbling on top of me. As the ball was sizzling towards the dugout, Voit reached over the railing and snagged the it. His momentum carried him right over the railing, falling headfirst into the trash can. He held onto the ball for the out. Now that is what a great ballplayer, hungry to make the big leagues, does - pedal to the metal.

His feet were dangling out of the trash can as he basically stood on his head. I must admit I was a little stunned, a little concerned for his well-being, and more than a little amused at the sight of him sticking upside down in the trash can. It all happened so fast. By the time I gathered my senses and knew everyone was safe, I was a little late getting the photo. By the time I snapped a shot he was mostly out of the can. Fortunately, the Springfield video crew did get it all on tape. Luke ended up going to Memphis the following year and made his Major League debut in 2017 at the tail end of the year.

Voit made it back to the parent club in 2018, seeing only limited playing time behind Jose Martinez. Before the start of one of our games in June, he was back in Springfield on a rehab assignment. As he walked down the right field line with his gear, he noticed me, walked over and tucked his bat and glove under his arm so we could shake hands. While he was stretching and playing catch, I was doing all my pre-game chores, like shooting first pitches and orchestrating the Field of Dreams team. Once the National Anthem was completed and the field cleared for the game to begin, I ran off the field and jumped into our dugout to get my camo hunting chair. I needed to get into position by the trash can. As I was looking out towards the field, I felt a gentle slap on the back. I turned around and it was Luke, who said hello again. I smiled and said: "Luke you still are the only Cardinal to end up head first in this trash can." He laughed and said, "Yeah, I kept waiting for my teammates to catch me, but they just watched" and let out a big laugh.

It was good to see Luke out on first base again. In the top of the second inning the opposing batter took a big swing and launched a high fly popup very similar to the one that put Luke in the trash can. It was heading towards the

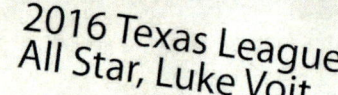

2016 Texas League All Star, Luke Voit.

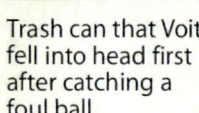

Trash can that Voit fell into head first after catching a foul ball.

Luke displays the knife he won for winning the H.R. derby.

Below:
Voit winning the 2016 Texas League All Star Homerun Derby, held in Springfield.

Cardinals dugout and towards the can. I heard that familiar sound of a freight train heading towards me and it instantly brought back memories. I thought, "Oh my gosh, Luke could end up in the trash can again." This time I had my camera ready all the time wondering what the odds would be if Luke went into the round file a second time. As the ball was sizzling downward into the dugout, Luke at the last second, pulled up short of the railing and let the ball drop safely into dugout, where it bounced off the trash can. Voit pointed his finger at me and said, "I'm not doing THAT again" and let out a big laugh. That is the difference between a youngster trying to make an impression and a veteran wanting to stay healthy. That was a good move on his part, because a few weeks later he was traded to the New York Yankees. He had only batted 11 times with St. Louis the entire first part of the year. When he was traded, the Yankees gave him the chance he needed to show off his talent. In 39 games with New York, he hit 14 home runs with a .322 batting average. He is on his way to stardom in the Big Apple.

CHAPTER 12
COMING OFF THE YIPS

In 1999 I was in St. Louis on business and was able to catch a game between the Cardinals and Padres. In the middle of the game a young pitching phenom, left hander Rick Ankiel, came into the game. He faced nine Padres that day and struck out eight of them. The only person to hit a fair ball was the great Tony Gwynn. On top of that, Rick had two strikes on him too. I have seen some great pitchers in person - Nolan Ryan, Roger Clemens, Bob Gibson, Pedro Martinez, Greg Maddox and Tom Seaver all come to mind. None of those pitchers were as dominate as Rick Ankiel that day. His pitching career soon took a twisted turn for the worse. In a playoff game against the Braves the next season and with one wild pitch, he had contracted what many people call "The Yips." It's an anxiety that is unexplainable, and devastating. There have been several major league players get the yips over the years. Steve Blass, the 1971 World Series hero for the Pirates, suffered from the same anxiety. Nothing was wrong with his arm, just his head. It doesn't happen to just pitchers. Steve Sax, All Star second basemen for the Dodgers had the yips every time he had to throw to first base. A routine throw to first base was his yips demon. I must admit, I know exactly how the yips feels.

I used to be a decent golfer. Usually shooting in the low to mid-80s. There was a par-three hole, in Wichita, Kan., that made my golf game go from decent to giving up the game for several years. It wasn't a difficult hole, only about 150 yards. My first ball went about three feet. Everybody laughed. The second, same thing. The third one went way off to the right. It got in my head. Every time I stood over the ball, I felt great, but there was a little voice that said I was going to mess up. And I did - a lot. I quit playing for twenty years. I have taken golf back up over the last three years and discovered that if I didn't care what my score was, the Yips went away. They are still there when I take a driver out of my golf bag, however.

In 2005 Ankiel was scheduled to join the Springfield Cardinals as an outfielder. He'd retired due to his anxiety issues, for about an hour. The Cardinals knew he was such a talented baseball player, not only pitching, but hitting and fielding as well. He was really our first marquee player in Springfield that everyone knew who he was. Fans were excited about him coming to town. Rick hurt his knee right before being promoted to Springfield from single A. We had to wait for his knee to heel up before we could see his trek back to the big leagues as an outfielder. He finally made it to town in May. Rick was standoffish. Whenever he saw a camera (mine) he seemed to always look the other way. I had the hardest time getting a good candid shot of him. He would not come out of the clubhouse until just about game time. The reason for that was he wanted to avoid fans. Rick had a small taste of greatness, and now he was fighting to earn a Double A outfield spot.

Over time he slowly got used to me being around. I think he realized I wasn't some paparazzi trying to sell shots of him to a tabloid. He hit a home run once and I timed the shot just right. After printing out the photo later that night, my plan was to give it to him before our next game. He was appreciative enough of the gesture, but there is no telling how many photos he has from his major league days.

Ankiel Returns

Rick Ankiel comes back to Hammons Field for a dinner in his honor in 2017.

Ankiel hit 10 hr's in just 34 games in Spfld during 2005.

Fans still talk about the throw Rick made from the center field track to nail a runner tagging from second base.

Nate Lucas interviews Ankiel about his struggles with Yips during a dinner on the infield.

Ankiel made Springfield lore on a throw he made to third base from centerfield during one of the games. There was a man on second base and the batter hit a deep fly ball to mid-warning track, about 400 feet from home. Ankiel drifted back to catch the ball, got his body into position to throw, and unleased a throw that has never been seen in Springfield before or since. The runner on second had tagged up on the fly and was headed for third. As the ball sailed towards third, I thought to myself, no way; nobody's capable of throwing a baseball like that. The runner slid into third just as the third baseman caught it over the bag, nailing the runner. The crowd went nuts. A few years later when Rick was back in the big leagues as an outfielder. I was watching the Cardinals play the Rockies on TV. During the game Ankiel made two throws in the same game just like the one he threw that day in Springfield. Both runners were out. The television announcers went crazy and said those were the best throws they had ever seen. I just laughed and shook my head and wondered how he could throw three strikes from the centerfield warning track to third base but could not come close from 60 feet 6 inches. The Yips are cruel. You can't feel too sorry for Ankiel. He ended up playing parts of 11 years in the majors, making a great living.

Rick came back to Hammons Field in 2017 after the regular season to promote a book and to attend a dinner in his honor. My task was to stay close to Ankiel. I was to take photos of him posing with dinner attendees. This time he was a different guy, very outgoing and pleasant. As I sat with him at his autograph table there was a little lull in the action. I told him that I was there the day he struck out eight out of nine Padres. He shook his head and said, "Yeah, I was on that day." It surprised me that he remembered that but when you think about it, he only pitched in parts of 51 major league games. After dinner he gave a very inspirational talk. He pointed out stories in his book, talking about how the yips had wrestled away his pitching career. The biggest point he made to the audience was that he is very much at peace. He has a beautiful wife and two great kids. Ankiel does some occasional commentary for the major-league Cardinals on television.

CHAPTER 13
WINTER CARAVAN

In mid-January every year the St Louis Cardinals send a contingent of people to Springfield to promote Cardinals baseball and the upcoming season. There are three or four different groups that spread out across Cardinal nation, traveling from town to town, shaking hands, speaking and signing autographs. When I was in junior high, I attended my first Cardinals caravan with my childhood friend Allen Smith. The event was held in the basement of the Lamplighter Inn in Springfield. As kids, we were starving for anything major-league related. There was an impressive line-up that traveled to Springfield that trip. Steve Carlton, Red Schoendienst, announcer Jay Randolph and Joe Hague. Each spoke for a few minutes and then signed autographs. Allen and I floated out of the room in total amazement that there were actual major league players in Springfield and that we got to meet them. The Kansas City Royals had a caravan a couple weeks later. Lou Piniella, Jerry May and manager Bob Lemon signed autographs at the Battlefield Mall. I remember hearing Lemon tell a fan that no one knows who he is and laughing. Lemon ended up being elected to the Major League Baseball Hall of Fame in 1976. He was an all-time great pitcher for the Cleveland Indians, but Springfield was and is a Cardinals town.

When the caravan first started to come to town after Springfield had a team, for some reason I never went. It might have been because the players coming to town were ones I didn't know personally. No one in the front office ever asked me to photograph any of the caravans until 2010. The 2012 Winter Caravan was a pretty special one. We were coming off one of the most exciting baseball seasons in years, with the Cardinals coming from 10-1/2 games behind in August to winning the World Series in dramatic fashion. It also was a season of change. Tony La Russa announced his retirement and Albert Pujols shocked Cardinals nation by signing with the Los Angeles Angels as a free agent. Transactions ripple through the entire system. Former Cardinals catcher Mike Matheny was hired to manage the club. He asked our old skipper Chris Maloney to coach first base, so that left an opening for a manager in Memphis. Pop Warner was coming off his fifth year as Springfield's manager and he got the promotion to Triple A. I was excited when they made the announcement that we were getting a new manager. Even though was not familiar with Mike Shildt I was impressing by all of the nice things people I did know were saying about him.

Springfield hit the caravan lottery that year. Traveling with the caravan were former Springfield Cardinals Jason Motte, who happened to be on the mound to close out the previous World Series; pitcher Mitchell Boggs, outfielder Shane Robinson and Matheny. St Louis is great about sending former players too. 1980's Cardinals pitching standout Danny Cox was in the group as well as 1990's pitcher Jason Simmontachi. The spokesperson for the caravan was broadcaster John Rooney. Each year, the caravan starts with a luncheon for our sponsors and vendors, held in the players locker room. That is a good place for me to say hello to guys that I know who passed through Springfield on their way up. My daughter Megan knew that Motte was coming to town and asked that I get him to sign something. After searching my old photo albums, I came across one of Jason. He had posed for me before a game with a big smile and a clean-shaven face.

After exchanging pleasantries, I handed Jason the photo to sign. He called Boggs and Robinson over to show them. He said, "This is the only photo I have seen of me where I was clean shaven." Jason said he had tried to trim a Fu Manchu mustache but messed it up, so he decided to shave it off and start over. That was the last time he had a clean grill. Jason signed the photo for my daughter. Even though he misspelled Megan by adding an a, she loved it.

After lunch there was a question and answer session in the training facility where two or three hundred fans flock to get a glimpse of players from their favorite team. Later that evening the players are shuttled to the campus of Missouri State, where they sat and watched the Bass Pro Tournament of Champions high school basketball tournament. During halftime, the players went to center court, while Rooney introduced them. After the introductions the players were escorted to a concourse where tables, pens, and photos were waiting. They signed hundreds of autographs. The grand finale this night was a private dinner on the second floor of a trendy restaurant called the Flying Tomato, on the Springfield public square.

Springfield staff was invited to attend the dinner. In my excitement, I arrived first to the restaurant. There was an open bar and I cracked open a Bud Light and sat at a table waiting for everyone to show up. I chose a table in the back, away from the action. Just being there was good enough for me. There was no need for me to take up space at the players' tables. Shortly, the crew started to walk in. Motte, Boggs, Robinson and Simmontachi were first to the party. It has always been my policy to not be a pest, nor a hanger-oner. I give players the space they need. Motte saw me in the corner and waved. He

2012 Cardinals Winter Caravan comes to Springfield.

Jason Simontacchi, Jason Motte, Mike Matheny, Mitchell Boggs, and Shane Robinson pose before dinner.

Motte told Boggs that this photo is the only one he has seen without his beard. Jason had messed up trimming his Fu manchu, so he started all over that day.

New St. Louis Cardinals manager Mike Matheny answers media questions in the Springfield players lounge.

Halftime introduction at the Tournament of Champions held at Missouri State University.

Cardinals Caravan 2010

Freese, Kinney, Hraboski waiting to be introduced.

Top row,L -R: Louie, Al Hraboski, David Freese, Kyle McClellan, Josh Kinny, Tom Pagnozzi   Front row L-R: John Roony, John Q Hammons, Kerry Robinson

proceeded to fix a few snacks, then made his way to my table and sat down, followed by Boggs, Robinson, and Simmontachi. My first thought was, I didn't want Gifford thinking I was horning in on their party, but he wasn't there to see I was the first one at the table. Those players made me feel like I was one of them, all on the same team. I thought that was pretty cool because they easily could have sat by themselves. Motte and Boggs were very friendly when they played in Springfield and we visited several times before games. Boggs told me his mom loved me. He said she bought tons of photos of Mitchell from my website. I told him that I loved her too. They started slamming a few beers, all the while including me in the conversation, which was appreciated.

I asked them how much crazier fans were since they had become known nationally after winning the World Series a few months earlier.

Motte told me a story about an autograph hound that kept asking for his autograph at a restaurant. He gave him a couple, but the guy had a handful of items he wanted signed. Jason said that he would only sign a couple things and went to his table. There was a bachelorette party dinner going on in the room. The autograph hound went over to the party and tried to bribe one of the party girls into taking a ball over to the bearded dude and ask him to sign it. She had no idea who Jason was. All the while this was going on, Jason was watching the autograph pest out of the corner of his eye. One of the girls reluctantly submitted to the pushy guy. She sheepishly walked over to Jason and asked if he would autograph the baseball. Jason said he told her the only way he would sign the ball was if she promised not to give it back to the hound. She laughed and agreed. Jason signed it, a limo was waiting, and all the girls jumped in, autographed ball and all. The autograph hound's eyes got big and he started chasing the limo on foot, yelling to give back his baseball.

Mitchell told a story of his own. He was leaving a bar with his wife when he was approached by a man holding out a baseball for him to sign. Mitchell was holding a beer in one hand and the ball in the other while signing it. During the brief encounter, the autograph seeker took a picture of Mitchell signing. A day or two went by before one of Mitchell's friends happened to be on eBay. The friend noticed that someone had put an autographed Mitchell Boggs baseball on eBay. What made it stick out was the picture he had posted to prove the signature was real. It was the picture of Boggs holding his beer, signing the ball. Boggs looked at me and said, "Can you believe he put that on eBay the next day?" He seemed upset over it. I said "Mitchell, that would not tick me off nearly as much as seeing a .99 cent starting bid, with no bids." Everyone got a pretty good laugh on that one.

Motte saw Danny Cox standing around so he and invited him to join our table. I was at game five of the 1987 World Series when Danny beat the Twins. In his book "You're Missing a Good Game" Whitely Herzog called Danny Cox the toughest player he ever managed. That's high praise coming from an old-school manger like the White Rat. We were about two hours into dinner and drinks, so it was best for me to gracefully bow out. As I was getting up from the table, Motte asked me to take a group shot of them. Matheny was at another table and saw what was going on, so he came over and photo bombed the group. This 2012 caravan was my best experience by far.

CHAPTER 14
PRE-SEASON PORTRAITS

The winter caravan is the first sign that a new baseball season is not too far down the road. When it gets time for the pre-season player portraits, winter has been defeated and spring is slowly taking over. Once spring training is over, and the roster has been finalized, players fly into Springfield to be introduced to the city, park, and staff. Management has a fan appreciation day for the players before the season starts. That's a good time to take a head and shoulders portrait of each player. A plain backdrop is set up with a couple strobe lights and a hair light. A plain background is used to make it easier to cut out the background and put whatever background our media department desires. We take them in a narrow hallway next to the media room upstairs on the third floor. It's tight quarters but I don't complain; we used to take them in a room the size of a closet. Once the portraits are taken, the players go next door to a video room where they will be videoed on a green screen. That video is used for scoreboard artwork. My photos have a few different uses; mainly they are for the St Louis Cardinals media guide, our scoreboard and media requests. As the years go by, our players look younger and younger. Heck, the manager and coaches look young to me these days.

Portrait day is a great time for me to introduce myself to all the newcomers, as well as greet players and coaches that I've already come to know. This has been a yearly tradition since our first year in existence. There is a system to our madness. A small group of four or five players will be ushered up to my portable studio. When each group arrives, I show them how to sit on the bar stool, where their feet go, and where they are to look. St Louis has a fair number of Latino players who don't speak much English, so I act out how they are supposed to pose. Speaking English loudly while I act it out makes no sense. I did purchase an app on my phone that translates English to Spanish. I fumble around with it and the players usually play along and wait for me to tell them something.

Everyone acts differently during a portrait shoot. Some players flash a big smile and boom, you have it. Usually I take a smiling as well as a serious pose. Some players will refuse to smile. They think they look Macho, but they just look mad to me. Other players want to see what the photo looks like and will request several to be taken until they are happy with it. Still others could care less. They smile or whatever and when I say "Next", they quickly leave. Coaches are the last to arrive for their photos. Some will say "use last year's" and not get one taken. That was a common occurrence when Pop Warner was manager. Dann Billardello managed here for a couple years. His request was to shoot him from the letters up - no stomach. He was only half kidding. Most of our coaches get theirs taken each year. The year my grandson Beau was born, in February of 2014, I wanted to do something for him that he would always have from his Pop's Harrell. I brought a baseball with me on portrait day to have the players sign before they had their photo taken. After looking at the signatures at the end of the day I realized that no one will know who signed the ball because you can't read the signatures. An idea popped into my head to print out our opening day roster and keep it with the ball. Then we would always know who signed the ball.

I have graduated to now having a bat signed each year by the players as I take their portraits. There probably are not many team autographed bats out there so these are special to me. The roster is always printed out and rubber band it around the bat, so we will know what players have signed it. I miss those days of beautifully signed autographs from guys like Mickey Mantle, Ted Williams, Hank Aaron and Stan Musial. Babe Ruth had a beautiful signature as well. He signed thousands and thousands of autographs, but I have yet to see one that looks like it was quickly scribbled. Those players took the time to not only write a legible signature but turn it into a piece of fine art. Today is a different time, and kids treasure those scribbles just like I treasured the old handiwork.

CHAPTER 15
GET A GRIP

Luke Gregerson was an up and coming late inning reliever when he joined Springfield at the start of the 2008 season. The first time I got to see him pitch was in the 9th inning of our preseason exhibition game against St. Louis. Luke does not throw hard but has great movement and good control. Outfielder Ryan Ludwig came to the plate for St. Louis to face Gregerson.

He delivered a pitch to Ludwig that slipped out of his hand and hit Ryan in the side of his helmet. Ludwig went down like a ton of bricks to the ground. There was a hush over the crowd as the St. Louis trainer went to his aid. Ludwig had a stunned look on his face as the trainer shined a flashlight into his eyes to see if his pupils were dilating. He ended up leaving the game. Gregerson was standing on the mound wanting to dig a hole and hide. He had just hit one of the leading homerun hitters for the Cardinals in the head, the day before the regular season was to begin. Fortunately, Ludwig was not seriously hurt.

Gregerson had a solid season in Springfield and went into the off season thinking he had a good shot at being promoted to Memphis. His plans were interrupted when he was part of a trade with the San Diego Padres for shortstop Khalil Greene. I was sad to see him go because Luke was a fun guy to be around. Fast forward to 2010. My wife Wendy and I were visiting my daughter Megan and her husband Grant in Tucson, Arizona during spring training. We decided to catch a game between the Padres and the Diamondbacks. As the players were walking out from the Padres clubhouse, I spotted Luke and called him

LUKEGREGERSON

never played a sport professionally. But when he played, he competed like a pro, even if just in local softball leagues.

"You're thinking, this guy's an animal," Gregerson says about watching him. "Why is he going so hard all the time?"

So his son became the type who always wanted the ball. Who never backed down.

And he was willing to put in the work, remembers Kyle McClellan, the former Cardinals pitcher who was Gregerson's teammate in the minors.

"Especially in the minor leagues, it's not always the case where guys are willing to put the work in. A lot of guys, their talent exceeds the level they're at, so they can just go out there and go through the motions and be the best guy on the field," explains McClellan. "From the very beginning, (Luke) was a guy who wasn't cutting corners, wasn't skimping out on the running or the weight lifting."

He also had some nasty tools. Gregerson didn't bring the heat, but boy, could he make the ball dance. Those who watched him pitch in the minors recall a power sinker and a swing-and-miss slider. Finding that identity, however, took some help from

When Gregerson couldn't come to grips with his slider in 2011 as a Padres reliever, he found other ways to get outs before solving the puzzle of his vanished weapon. He discovered the clue – his thumb position – on a baseball card from his days as a Cardinals minor leaguer.

Johnson City pitching coach Al Holland. To this day, 10 seasons into his major league career, Gregerson describes one revelatory meeting with Holland as a "game-changer."

It came just a couple weeks after he'd been drafted. As he transitioned into his pro career, Gregerson had been throwing four-seam fastballs, which were being hit everywhere. Because he'd never been a high-velocity guy, he didn't have a pitch he could blow past batters even at the rookie-league level.

One day, Holland took him aside.

"We've got to get you something that moves," the coach insisted.

He began showing Gregerson multiple grips, but to no avail: the ball kept sailing straight and narrow. Finally, Gregerson volunteered a grip he'd used in college. He threw it once. It had good, hard sink.

Holland stepped back.

"Cuz, you've got to throw that *every time!*" he exclaimed.

Gregerson credits that "discovery" and encouragement with helping him move rapidly through the minors. His performance at high-A Palm Beach in 2007 and Double-A Springfield in '08 resulted in appearances in

each league's All-Star game. The next spring, he made a major league Opening Day roster – only not with St. Louis.

Heading into the 2009 season, the Cardinals moved to add more offense at shortstop by acquiring Khalil Greene from the Padres for pitcher Mark Worrell and a player to be named. The player turned out to be Gregerson.

The trade worked out well for the budding righthander – his inclusion on the Padres' season-opening roster launched a big-league career that spanned San Diego, Oakland and Houston. During those nine seasons, he held righthanded batters to the fifth-lowest batting average (.200) in the majors among qualified relievers. He also accumulated the third-most appearances (363) in Padres history.

Used with permission from Cardinals Gameday Magazine.

In 2018 Luke Gregerson made a rehabilitation appearance in Springfield.

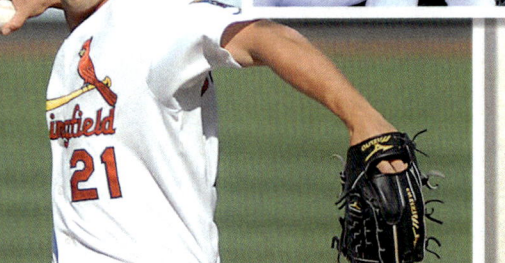

This is the original photo used for Gregerson's 2008 baseball card set.

over to say hello. He came over and I reminded him of the time he hit Ludwig in the head. He rolled his eyes and said "La Russa was in the dugout and I saw him jump up when Ryan was hit and all I could think about was; there goes my career". We both had a laugh on that one. I told him that we were all proud of him back in Springfield and then went back to my seat.

In 2018 St. Louis signed Gregerson to a two-year contract bringing him back to the Cardinals. He pitched for a couple months with St. Louis having mixed results. The *Cardinals Game Day Magazine* had written a feature story on him. The meat of the story was how Gregerson had tasted major league success with San Diego, Oakland, and Houston, and had finally came full circle back to St. Louis. There was one part of the story that captured my attention right away. It was a picture of a 2008 Springfield Cardinals baseball card of Luke. The caption read, "When Gregerson couldn't come to grips with his slider in 2011 as a Padres reliever, he found other ways to get outs before solving the puzzle of his vanished weapon. He discovered the clue – his thumb position – on a baseball card from his days as a Cardinals minor leaguer." I had taken the photo on that card!

Luke injured his shoulder during the first part of the 2018 season which resulted in him being assigned to Springfield for two game rehabilitation assignment. It's always fun to see players return to Hammons that I haven't seen for a while. I always wonder in the back of my mind if they will remember me. I got my answer quickly from Gregerson. He came walking in from the bullpen during pregame, came over and shook my hand and we exchanged pleasantries. A couple of years ago St. Louis instituted a rule with bullpen pitchers that require them to remain in the dugout for the first three innings of a game. After that; they are to go down to the bullpen for the remainder of the game unless called upon. I walked over to Luke in our dugout before the game started and told him that I had read the article about him in *Cardinals Game Day Magazine*. I pointed out that the photo on the baseball card that revived his career was taken by me. He thought for a second and then his face lit up and he said, "Oh yeah, that's right!" I playfully held out my hand like I was asking for money. He got all fake serious, shook his head and said, "Talk to my agent!" I told him "Don't worry about it. It was payment enough for me to know that my photo saved your career." I said, tongue in cheek...

CHAPTER 16
CHAMPIONSHIP RING

John Mozeliak, the Cardinals' president of baseball
operations, comes to Springfield a few times each season
to watch prospects and get a feel for how our team is
doing. A perk of winning a World Series is being presented
with a World Series ring. They are handed out to players,
coaches and staff. St. Louis also hands out rings to their
minor league staff as a symbol of their gratitude for
helping mold players and get them ready for the major
leagues. The spring after the Cardinals won the 2011
World Series, Mozeliak came to town to present the
Springfield staff with World Series rings. Matt Gifford had
asked if I could take photos of the ceremony, being held
up in the Champions Lounge on the third floor. The staff
gathered around while John made a speech on how
exciting it was to have Springfield as part of the
organization and how important we were to the
development of future Cardinals major league players and
coaches. As he handed out the rings to staff, I've got to
admit I was a little jealous. What a family heirloom that
ring would be. Because I am contracted, and not an actual
employee, I was not eligible for a St. Louis ring. After the
rings were handed out, Mozeliak shared some inside
baseball with us about plans and strategies.

The ceremony was right before the beginning of the 2012
season. We had a new manager as Shildt was replacing
Warner. Mike had been a scout before turning to
managing a few years earlier. He never played a day of
professional baseball but had been around baseball his
entire life. We were all excited about 2012 because we

Championship Rings

Jeff Levering (center) being presented his 2011 World Series ring by Matt Gifford (l) and then General Manager of the St. Louis Cardinals, John Mozeliak (R)

My proudest Springfield Cardinals moment is being awarded a 2011 Texas League Championship Ring.

Matt Gifford, Mark Harrell, Mike Shildt

had heard there were several future major leaguers that would be playing in Springfield that season.

Oscar Taveras, Kolten Wong, Trevor Rosenthal, Seth Maness and Carlos Martinez headlined an impressive roster. There were some later additions at the end of the season that helped push the team to the finish line like pitcher Michael Wacha and outfielder Mike O'Neill. During that season there were 25 players who played at least one game for Springfield that went on to play in the major leagues. That included a three-game rehabilitation assignment for Matt Carpenter.

The Cardinals' most successful season remains the 2012 campaign, during which they finished first in the North Division in the second half, posted a division-best and franchise mark with a 77-61 record and won the Texas League championship, defeating the Tulsa Drillers 3-2 in the best-of-five divisional playoff round before winning the title in a best-of-five series against the Frisco Roughriders. The championship game was played in Frisco, Texas. Sadly, I did not make that trip. I would have loved to have gotten photos of the celebration at home plate after the win. I did get some great shots of the players celebrating after the Northern Division victory. That was the step before winning it all. Gifford confided in me later that it had slipped his mind to ask me to go to Texas for the championship game. He promised me if the team got in that position in the future, he would make sure and take me. 2012 was indeed a special team and a magical year.

The 2013 season was still a few weeks out when I received a call from Gifford. When I saw who was on the telephone I wondered why Matt was calling. Most of the communication I had with Matt was either through texts or emails. When I answered, the first thing he asked me was what was my ring size. I was a little bit stunned and didn't know how to answer that. He said, "The reason I'm asking you is because you are going to get a 2012 Texas Championship ring." To say I was overwhelmed with emotion would be an understatement. I told him I would have to go to Walmart and get measured, then laughed. Gifford didn't have to give me a ring. He recommended to St. Louis that I be awarded one. It was a gesture I will never forget and always be thankful for. A few weeks later the new rings came into the office. I received an invitation to come out and shoot the Texas League Championship ring ceremony. Only this time, I needed to recruit someone to take my picture when my turn came. My ring has "Harrell" in bold letters along one side along with a classy design that pays tribute to the championship season over the rest of the ring. When I got home and showed my family the ring, my son Ryan joked, "I get that ring when you're dead." I told him of course he would. My son-in-law Grant asked if he could have the wooden box the ring came in because it would be useful to put spare change in. It is so nice to be loved by everyone.

ACKNOWLEDGEMENTS

This book has been begging to jump out of my head and onto paper for about six years. With no prior knowledge about writing a book, the thought did intimidate me. It's actually a fortunate thing that I waited so long to write this. Online technology in self-publishing makes it easier for a writer to get published. During conversations with friends, fans and family, I often told a fun baseball story and they would get a kick out of it. One story led to another and another. The reaction was always the same – "You should write a book." During dinner after a winter caravan event even Cardinals legend Al Hrabosky told me I should write a book. He has seen me at several games throughout the years and thought it would be a good idea.

This book would never have been written if my wife Wendy had not supported me, or at least tolerated my massive time away from home during evenings and weekends, shooting Cardinals baseball for 14 years. Number 15 is right around the corner. She became a baseball wife in a way. Except I was home every night after the game and was not making the money professional ballplayers make. I want to thank her for her patience. She works hard at her job and it is stressful at times for her. Yet she keeps our home in order. Thank you for that dear. It was a lot to ask of her to spend so many nights at home while I was running up and down those stairs at Hammons Field. She would attend two or three games a year, usually with my bonus daughter Samantha and bonus son Brandon. That is enough for her. The past several years Wendy has grown to like watching the St. Louis Cardinals on TV. Occasionally when I come home, the St. Louis game will be on the TV and she will be sitting there watching. That's pretty cool.

There would be no book if I had not been given to opportunity to be the official photographer of the Springfield Cardinals. I owe a great debt of gratitude to Matt Gifford who gave me the opportunity to feel like part of the family all these years. These memories will last the rest of my life. Matt is now working for the St. Louis Cardinals in the front office. His replacement, Dan Reiter, was the very last staff hire in 2005, our inaugural season. He went from last hire to VP and General Manager in mid-2017. Thanks Dan, for allowing me to continue this streak, capturing Springfield history. Thanks to Rob and Sally Rains for asking over the last few years how my book was coming along, motivating me to get this done. Rob offered to edit it, which was greatly appreciated. I want to thank my non-blood cousin Randy Hinton, and his wife Suzanne, who's my blood cousin. They were kind enough to help with editing pages too. You can blame them for typos. There are so many staff, sponsors, loyal fans and stadium workers that it is impossible to name them, but they will be a part of my Cardinal family forever. You know, this really is a pretty sweet gig.

Birds other than Cardinals

(R) This shot was taken during a fifteen minute hawk delay

(Far R) Drillers players fed a baby dove in their dugout during a game.

There have been hawk delays at Hammons Field. Our resident momma hawk is an impresive sight to see. Magneuris Sierra keeps a nervous eye on Mama Hawk.

It was so hot one game a pidgeon refused to leave until she had her fill of water from the groundskeepers hose.

First Professional Game at Busch III
Springfield vs. Memphis

Maloney shakes hands with Brendan Ryan.

Springfield on the field at Busch III.

Former Springfield Cards
Hanson , Kinney, Estrada

Former Spfld. Cards Shaun Boyd
is greeted by Memphis teammates
after hitting the first professional
homer in Busch Stadium III history.

Fun Around Hammons Field

(L) Allen Craig sitting with fans waiting his turn during home run derby.

(Below) Players blowing off some steam during a rain delay practicing "The Worm".

(Above) Players zoning in while a relief pitcher is warming up.

(R) Jason Simontacchi, Jobel Jimenez, and Sandy Alcantara model their groovy jersey's.

First Springfield Cardinal to be promoted to St. Louis.

Top:
Josh Kinney closing out a game for Springfield in 2005. My camera equipment at that time was not good for low light. Late inning relievers were always a challenge to get. Now the challenge is to stay late enough to see them pitch.

Bottom:
Kinney (with Signman photo bombing) is proudly holding his daughter Star, while getting ready to throw out a first pitch to Adam Wainwright, during an exhibition game between St. Louis, and Springfield, to open the 2017 season.

Andrew Knizner 2018

Matt Carpenter hit .316
for Springfield in 2010.

Below:
Carpenter & Brandon
Moss on rehab here
in 2016.
Moss asked Carp
why the crowd only
cheered for him?

On their way up...

Greg Garcia 2012

Aledmys Diaz 2014

Daniel Descalso 2008

Tony Cruz 2009

Tyler Greene 2007

Brendan Ryan 2005

Harrison Bader   Paul Dejong   Carson Kelly

Bader 2016

Paul Dejong 2016

On their way up...

Andrew Brown 2009

Colby Rasmus 2007

Xavier Scruggs 2010

Matt Adams 2011

Kolten Wong 2012

Pete Kozma 2009

Opposing Players Destined for the Big Leagues.

Top: Mike Moustakas
Northwest Arkansas Naturals

Nolan Arenado, Tulsa Drillers

Lower Middle (R): Mike Trout
Arkansas Travelers

Kyle McClellan
Frisco Roughriders (former Cardinal)

Alex Gordon, Wichita Wranglers

Pitchers on their way up.

Matt Pearce, Austin Gomber, Sandy Alcantara, Dakota Hudson, Jack Flaherty

(R) Gomber 2017

Flaherty 2017

Hudson 2017

Pitchers on their way up.

Carlos Martinez 2012
Mitchell Boggs 2007
Sam Freeman 2009

Seth Maness 2012
Jaime Garcia 2007
Alex Reyes 2015

Pitchers on their way up.

Shelby Miller 2011
Luke Weaver 2016
Adam Ottavino 2008

Joe Kelly 2011
Sandy Alcantara 2017
Trevor Rosenthal 2012

Promotions

Adam
Wainwright
on a rehab
assignment
in 2018

Waino throws another
shutout inning.

Walk Off Wins 2018

Above: Randy Arozarena
hits walk off homerun.

Center; Jeremy Martinez
celebrates his game
winning single .

Below: Johan Mieses gets
a wet greeting after a walk
off HR.

Clubhouse walls awaiting new additions.

Players past and present have stopped to look at these photos on their way to the indoor workout facilities.